OECD Guidelines on Measuring Subjective Well-being (2025 Update)

OECD
BETTER POLICIES FOR BETTER LIVES

Please cite this publication as:
OECD (2025), *OECD Guidelines on Measuring Subjective Well-being (2025 Update)*, OECD Publishing, Paris, https://doi.org/10.1787/9203632a-en.

ISBN 978-92-64-72004-6 (print)
ISBN 978-92-64-34118-0 (PDF)
ISBN 978-92-64-92121-4 (HTML)

Photo credits: Cover © Black Salmon/Shutterstock.com.

Corrigenda to OECD publications may be found at: https://www.oecd.org/en/publications/support/corrigenda.html.

Foreword

OECD measurement guidelines support the organisation's work in advancing the measurement of concepts that are crucial to the well-being of people, the planet and future generations. Beginning with the publication of the first edition of the *OECD Guidelines on Measuring Subjective Well-being* in 2013, the organisation has provided data producers with survey modules and best practices when capturing data on topics as diverse as micro-statistics on household wealth; the distribution of household income, consumption and wealth; trust; the quality of the working environment; and population mental health. This work contributes to the OECD's on-going efforts to measure and monitor progress in multidimensional well-being across OECD member states. Measurement guidelines enhance the harmonisation of well-being metrics and enable cross-country comparisons. The OECD *How's Life? Well-being Database* (available online here: http://data-explorer.oecd.org/s/fu and updated on a quarterly basis) includes 80+ indicators that provide information on current well-being outcomes, well-being inequalities, and the resources and risks that underpin future well-being.

This report was prepared by the OECD Centre on Well-being, Inclusion, Sustainability and Equal Opportunity (WISE). Jessica Mahoney was the lead author, with editorial oversight from Lara Fleischer and Carrie Exton. The work was carried out under the direction of Romina Boarini. Martine Zaïda, Taylor Kelly and Anne-Lise Faron provided support throughout on communication co-ordination and formatting. Patrick Hamm copy-edited the volume.

An informal advisory group, chaired by Carrie Exton (OECD, WISE), provided extensive feedback and valuable comments throughout the process of drafting this report. We are grateful to the members of the informal advisory group: Matías Cociña (Ministry of Social Development and Family, Government of Chile), Jason Fields (United States Census Bureau), Rosemary Goodyear (Statistics New Zealand), Carol Graham (Brookings Institution), John Helliwell (University of British Columbia), Emily Hewlett (OECD, Directorate for Employment, Labour and Social Affairs), Nancy Hey (Lloyd's Register Foundation), Erhabor Idemudia (North-West University), Yosuke Kono (Cabinet Office, Government of Japan), Noémie Le Donné (OECD, Education Directorate), Timothy Lomas (Harvard University), Shigehiro Oishi (University of Chicago), Anna Pärnänen (Statistics Finland), Gwyther Rees (UNICEF Innocenti Center), Mariano Rojas (Tecnológico Nacional de México), Carol Ryff (University of Wisconsin-Madison), Francesco Sarracino (National Institute of Statistics and Economic Studies of Luxembourg (STATEC)), Claudia Senik (CEPREMAP, l'Observatoire du Bien-être), Conal Smith (Kōtātā Insights), Arthur Stone (University of Southern California), Laura Taylor (University of Oxford), Olivier Thévenon (OECD, WISE) Atawhai Tibble (Indigenous Economist), Alessandra Tinto (Italian National Institute of Statistics), Sabrina Twilhaar (University of Warwick) and Anna Visser (Department of the Taoiseach, Government of Ireland). Advisory group members provided helpful feedback and guidance throughout the process; however, the final recommendations are those put forth by the Secretariat, with oversight from delegates of the OECD Committee on Statistics and Statistical Policy (CSSP) and may not reflect the personal views of each advisory group member.

This work also benefitted from the expertise of external consultants who were contracted to produce working papers on measuring specific aspects of subjective well-being: Laura Kudrna (University of Birmingham), Tharuka Nanomi Arachchige (University of Birmingham), Lailah Alidu (University of Birmingham) and Paul Dolan (London School of Economics) (affect); Saamah Abdallah (Hot or Cool Institute) (eudaimonia); and Conal Smith (Kōtātā Insight), Margreet Freiling (Kōtātā Insight) and Hinako Percival (Kōtātā Insight and Massey University) (globally inclusive approaches to measurement). We additionally thank the engagement and helpful comments of Jason Adams, Richard Archambault and Patrick Bussiere (Employment and Social Development Canada); Alden Lai (New York University School of Global Public Health); Lucía Macchia (University of London); Frank Martela (Aalto University); Kelsey O'Connor (National Institute of Statistics and Economic Studies of Luxembourg (STATEC)); Eoin O'Mahony and Fiona Bourke (Economic Division, Department of the Taoiseach); Andrew Oswald (University of Warwick); and Joar Vittersø (University of Tromsø).

These *Guidelines* were produced as part of the work programme of the OECD Committee on Statistics and Statistical Policy (CSSP), whose delegates have reviewed the report and provided comments. Their contributions and advice are gratefully acknowledged.

Support for this report was provided in part by the Well-being for Planet Earth Foundation.

Table of contents

Tables

Figures

Boxes

Executive summary

Subjective well-being data complement objective measures of well-being by providing important information on how people perceive their life experiences

Subjective well-being data reveal how people think about and experience their lives. Each component of subjective well-being – *life evaluation* (reflective assessments, such as satisfaction with life), *affect* (feelings or emotional states) and *eudaimonia* (a sense of worth, meaning and purpose) – captures a distinct and meaningful facet of people's subjective life experiences. These data serve as an important complement to objective measures of economic and social progress and can yield policy-relevant insights when collected and analysed in a rigorous manner. Subjective well-being data should be among the outcomes considered when monitoring social trends and benchmarking broad societal progress. These data are intrinsically important but can also serve as an early warning sign for developments in other well-being outcomes and thus can support policy design and evaluation – for example, to inform strategic planning, performance frameworks and budgeting processes.

This second edition of the *OECD Guidelines on Measuring Subjective Well-being* updates guidance for data producers interested in measuring subjective well-being in a statistically sound manner in line with good international practice

The first edition of the *OECD Guidelines on Measuring Subjective Well-being*, published in 2013, provided data producers with the evidence and tools they need to measure subjective well-being in official statistics. The 2013 *Guidelines* sought to improve the quality and usefulness of subjective well-being data in several ways: by providing explicit instructions on question wording, answer scales and survey implementation details; by giving guidance to data users on how to best analyse subjective well-being data; and, ultimately, by enhancing the international comparability of subjective well-being statistics. Ten years on, the profile of subjective well-being data in official statistics has grown considerably: close to 90% of OECD member states collect life satisfaction data in nationally representative household surveys. While international practice has converged around a standard measure of life satisfaction, there are still differences in current approaches to measuring affect and eudaimonia.

This second edition of the OECD *Guidelines* builds on the foundation of the first edition. It reiterates some of the measurement recommendations and best practices first outlined in 2013, while clarifying and streamlining recommendations in some areas to enhance their relevance and value in light of new policy demands and research results. This edition pulls in new evidence that has been published in the intervening decade, including practical findings from national statistical office measurement practice, to make updated recommendations that are designed to increase the inclusion of subjective well-being measures in official data, move towards greater convergence in measurement practice at the international level, and enhance the usefulness of subjective well-being for policy. The core module has been shortened but retains two measures – one on satisfaction with life, and one on the sense that that the things one does in life are worthwhile – and it introduces a new measure on pain. Other updates in this edition include a refined definition of eudaimonia, which more clearly illustrates the constructs to be included in this measurement module. A clearer distinction between affect and mental health measures is also made, along with guidance on when to use the two approaches. This edition also expands advice in other areas to account for advances in the evidence base and to enhance the global relevance of the recommended measures. Experimental measures, newly introduced in this volume, cover measures of subjective well-being with a strong relational component, such as balance and harmony in one's life, a connection to future generations and an emotional connection to the natural world.

Recommended question modules can be tailored based on user needs

This report contains the following practical resources to support survey designers and statistical agencies to capture data on subjective well-being in household and time use surveys, regardless of how far advanced their current measurement practice is:

- A shortened core module of three priority subjective well-being measures
- Streamlined extended modules for each component of subjective well-being, including resources for time use surveys
- A new, cross-cutting experimental module and three experimental question banks

Each survey module is accompanied by detailed implementation instructions, outlining the anticipated length of the module and practical guidance for enumerators, information on the original source of measures, and instructions for how to report the resulting data. The introductory chapter shares general good practice in subjective well-being measurement that is applicable to each of the survey modules that follow, covering topics such as survey design, sampling and target population, mode, question phrasing and placement, answer scale formulation, and data analysis and interpretation. Detailed information on the process of updating the *OECD Guidelines* and evidence supporting the updates and changes made to specific modules are described at length in the report Annex.

1. Measuring subjective well-being

This chapter introduces OECD work to standardise international measurement practices for key concepts that are instrumental in understanding what makes a good life. It provides a working definition of subjective well-being and its components – life evaluation, affect and eudaimonia – and establishes the importance and relevance of measuring these outcomes in official surveys. Specific updates to measurement recommendations in this edition of the *Guidelines* are highlighted, namely: (1) a shortened core module, (2) streamlined extended modules of each component of subjective well-being and (3) a new cross-cutting module of experimental measures and question banks for the experimental concepts. The chapter concludes with an overview of good measurement practice, touching on topics relating to survey design and methodology, question phrasing and placement, answer scale formulation, and data analysis and reporting.

Subjective well-being encompasses the ways that people experience and think about their lives. It is a core component of people's broader well-being, which the OECD has measured since 2011 using a multidimensional framework that encompasses a variety of economic, social and environmental outcomes. Subjective well-being outcomes not only are meaningfully associated with objective health, education and labour market outcomes (for example), but also shed light on trends in how people subjectively assess their experiences – which may diverge from trends in other measures of progress in meaningful ways. Incorporating subjective well-being data into countries' processes of monitoring and benchmarking their well-being progress, and in designing and evaluating their policy programmes, provides an important complement to objective measures of economic, social and environmental progress (OECD, 2013[1]).

The first *OECD Guidelines on Measuring Subjective Well-being* were published in 2013 (OECD, 2013[1]), following the launch of the OECD Well-being Framework and the associated Better Life Initiative in 2011 (OECD, 2011[2]). This work was borne out of the Stiglitz-Sen-Fitoussi Commission, which centred on the necessity of moving beyond GDP when measuring and assessing societal progress (Stiglitz, Sen and Fitoussi, 2009[3]). The Commission report explicitly recommended collecting subjective well-being measures in official statistics, noting that these questions provide meaningful and valid data about key aspects of people's quality of life. The follow-up report devoted a full chapter to subjective well-being measurement, with recommendations for next steps to improve uptake (Stiglitz, Fitoussi and Durand, 2018[4]). In 2013, few OECD countries were collecting data on subjective well-being in official statistics, and those that did were not necessarily doing so in standardised ways.

Thus, the original *Guidelines* sought to synthesise the existing body of evidence on subjective well-being measures in an easy-to-read format, with practical recommendations for national statistics offices and other interested data producers. The goals were four-fold: to improve the *quality* of subjective well-being data through recommendations on question wording and survey design, to improve the *usefulness* of the data by outlining methodological best practices, to increase the *harmonisation* of international statistics by converging practice around a core set of measures and to provide *guidance* to data users when analysing subjective well-being data.

Following the publication of the first iteration of the *OECD Guidelines*, the practice of collecting subjective well-being data in official surveys markedly increased in OECD countries. By 2023, close to 90% of OECD countries collected data on life satisfaction in nationally representative household surveys (with over 80% doing so annually), and over half included a measure of subjective well-being in national well-being initiatives (Mahoney, 2023[5]). Regular tracking of outcomes throughout the COVID-19 pandemic and the cost-of-living crisis yielded compelling insights into how aspects of subjective well-being were impacted by these shocks and how well these were able to rebound – or not – in the ensuing months and years (OECD, 2021[6]; What Works Wellbeing, 2021[7]; Perona, 2025[8]). Indeed, there has been growing attention to the importance of subjective well-being data both to understand how people in OECD countries are navigating the complex challenges facing citizens and policy makers alike, including the digital transition, increasing geopolitical instability and conflict, climate change and the transition to net zero, and to better understand the structural changes that have contributed to deteriorating outcomes for younger people.

This second edition of the *OECD Guidelines on Measuring Subjective Well-being* builds off the measurement recommendations and best practices published in the 2013 edition. It re-affirms the importance of measuring subjective well-being in official statistics and provides interested data producers with the information and tools they need to measure subjective well-being in a robust, well-validated and internationally comparable way. These updated *Guidelines* provide continuity for those data producers who took on board the recommendations outlined in the first edition, while clarifying recommendations in some areas to increase take-up, and expanding recommendations in other areas to account for developments in the evidence base in the intervening decade. More specifically, the second edition of the *Guidelines* makes three key changes from the first, by introducing:

- A shortened core module of priority subjective well-being measures (Box 2.2).

- Streamlined extended modules for each component of subjective well-being (Box 2.3 – Box 2.8).
- A new, cross-cutting experimental module and experimental question banks (Box 3.1 and Table 3.1 – Table 3.3); this provides a useful resource to data producers interested in expanding their coverage of subjective well-being elements that have thus far been under-measured.

Forthcoming OECD work will provide additional recommendations for measuring subjective well-being in children and young people.

This introductory chapter defines *what* subjective well-being is and *why* it should be measured. It provides more detailed information on which aspects of these guidelines have been updated, as well as important methodological and measurement considerations that apply to the collection of all subjective well-being data, regardless of which modules or measures survey designers choose to integrate.

Chapters 2 and 3 provide specific modules of subjective well-being measures that can be integrated into existing household and time use surveys. Chapter 2 introduces a series of recommended survey modules: a core module of subjective well-being, followed by extended modules that narrow in on specific component areas (life evaluation, domain evaluation, affect, eudaimonia and population mental health); three modules for time use surveys are also included. Chapter 3 provides a cross-cutting module of experimental subjective well-being measures, followed by three question banks for important topics for which the statistical evidence base is still emerging. In both chapters, each module is presented alongside detailed implementation instructions so as to provide enumerators and survey designers with the contextual information needed to field these measures and interpret the resulting data in a robust way. Additional information supporting measure selection can be found in Annex A.

Defining subjective well-being

Subjective well-being refers to the ways in which people experience and evaluate their own lives. More specifically, the OECD defines subjective well-being as:

> *Good mental states, including all of the various evaluations, positive and negative, that people make of their lives and the affective reactions of people to their experiences.*

This broad definition, initially put forth in the first edition of the *Guidelines*, includes different concepts housed under the general umbrella of subjective well-being. It provides space for cognitive evaluations that people make of their lives, for hedonic dimensions of human experience, and for concepts relating to living well, having good psychological functioning and making the most of one's talents and capacities. This definition is distinct from *well-being* more broadly defined (Box 1.1). Subjective well-being is also a distinct concept in its own right; its definition does not extend to *any and all* perception-based indicators (for example, a household's assessment of facing financial difficulties, or trust in government); nor does it encompass all *self-reported* indicators, some of which can still refer to objectively observable conditions (for example, self-reported income).

Box 1.1. Multidimensional well-being measurement at the OECD

Well-being, as set out in the OECD's Well-being Framework, is a multidimensional construct that encompasses the key outcomes that matter to people's lives, spanning material conditions, quality of life, and relational and environmental aspects (Figure 1.1). Subjective well-being, then, is a *component* of broader well-being, to be assessed alongside other measures including income, health, knowledge and skills, safety, environmental quality and social connections.

In addition to serving as a tool to benchmark country progress and shape policy analysis, the OECD's Well-being Framework also highlights gaps in the evidence base, thereby guiding OECD efforts to improve the availability, frequency and cross-country comparability of key concepts relevant to well-being. The 2013 subjective well-being publication was the first of the OECD's measurement guidelines, but in the years since, the organisation has published recommendations for official data producers on many other topics, including: micro-statistics on household wealth (OECD, 2013[9]); the distribution of household income, consumption and wealth (OECD, 2013[10]); trust (OECD, 2017[11]); the quality of the working environment (OECD, 2017[12]); and population mental health (OECD, 2023[13]) (refer to Box A A.1 for a discussion on how mental health outcomes relate to subjective well-being). Forthcoming work will focus on social connections (see Box A A.2 for more details on how this work relates to subjective well-being measurement).

Figure 1.1. OECD Well-being Framework

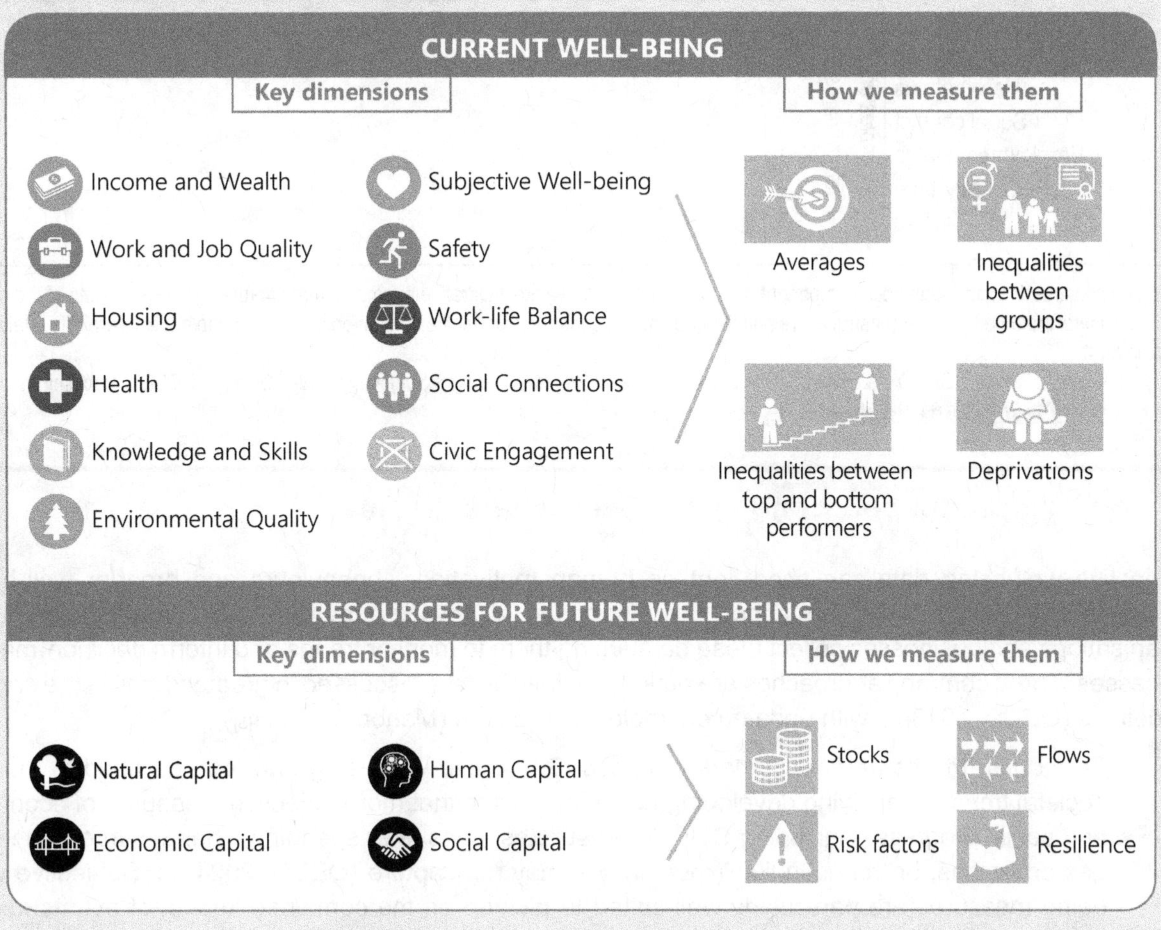

Source: OECD (2024[14]), *How's Life? 2024: Well-being and Resilience in Times of Crisis*, OECD Publishing, Paris, https://doi.org/10.1787/90ba854a-en.

To help clarify how the different components of subjective well-being relate to one another, and the underlying factors that shape these outcomes, the original guidelines proposed a conceptual framework of subjective well-being (Figure 1.2). Subjective well-being contains three distinct components: life evaluation, affect and eudaimonia. Each component has intrinsic value, and approaches to subjective well-being measurement should ideally capture all three.

- *Life evaluation* is a reflective assessment on a person's life or some specific aspect of it.
- *Affect* refers to a person's feelings or emotional states, typically measured with reference to a particular point in time.
- *Eudaimonia* is broadly defined as a feeling that one is living well, and pertains to whether individuals perceive that the things they do in life are worthwhile and have meaning, and whether they feel competent and autonomous and have a sense of personal growth and self-acceptance.

Figure 1.2. A conceptual framework of subjective well-being

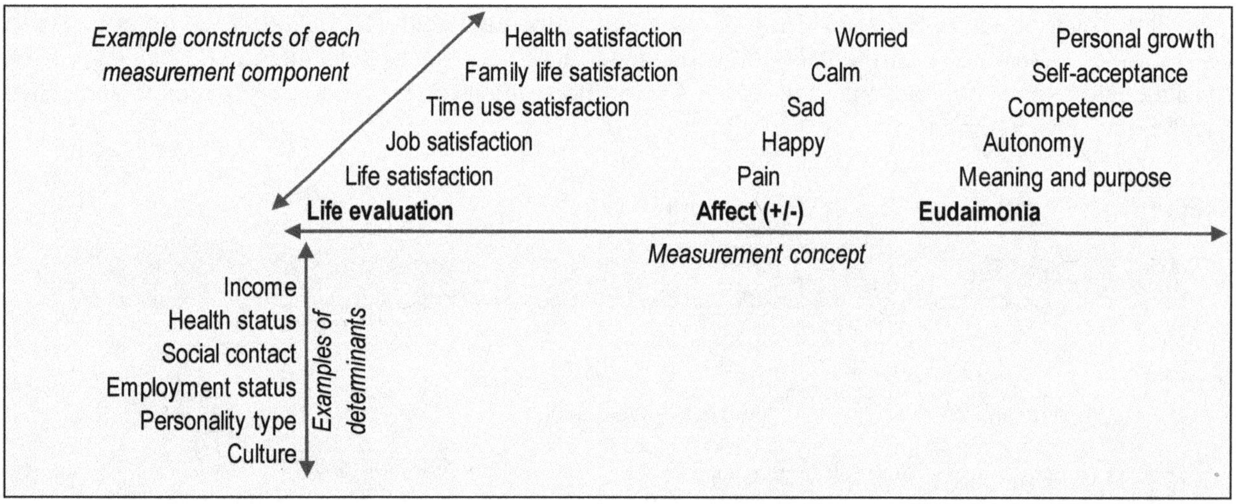

Note: The constructs listed within each component of subjective well-being are illustrative examples that capture different aspects of the overall concept; it is *not* assumed that the constructs are additive (i.e. that all constructs under life evaluation are summed to equal overall life evaluation, for example).
Source: Adapted from OECD (2013[1]), *OECD Guidelines on Measuring Subjective Well-being*, OECD Publishing, Paris, https://doi.org/10.1787/9789264191655-en.

The policy case for collecting subjective well-being data

Subjective well-being data can shed light on human motivations, behaviours and broader well-being outcomes that policy makers care about. For this reason, a growing number of governments, community organisations and businesses collect these data, using them to monitor trends and inform decision-making processes. Three common approaches are outlined below, but are discussed in greater detail in the original guidelines (OECD, 2013[1]), with updated examples provided in (Mahoney, 2023[5]).

- *To monitor trends and benchmark progress.* Subjective well-being data can be used to monitor societal trends, identifying developing points of tension that more objective measures of economic and social progress – including GDP, interest rates, consumer spending, changes in greenhouse gas emissions, or trends in life expectancy – may not capture (OECD, 2024[14]). Subjective well-being measures are particularly well-suited to pick up on the combined impact of events across multiple domains of life (Delhey and Kroll, 2012[15]), and they can help identify other relevant drivers – such as interpersonal relationships, availability of leisure time and community life – that may otherwise be neglected in discussions of societal progress. Trends in life evaluation, affect and eudaimonia may reveal important societal developments, such as dissatisfaction with the status quo, that objective measures of economic performance do not pick up, and policy makers who do not measure the former may miss important signs of growing dissatisfaction or unrest (Ianchovichina, 2018[16]; Hadzi-Vaskov and Ricci, 2021[17]). Subjective well-being data can also help to shed light on the full extent of the impacts of socio-economic hardship (Ryff, 2024[18]; Morozink et al., 2025[19]).

- *To serve as an early warning sign for other well-being outcomes.* The evidence base has established that subjective well-being outcomes today – such as life satisfaction, positive affect, hope, and meaning and purpose in life – are heavily correlated with certain objective outcomes in the future (Kaiser and Oswald, 2022[20]), in particular those relating to physical and mental health (Chida and Steptoe, 2008[21]; Cohen et al., 2006[22]; Graham and Pinto, 2019[23]; Cohen, Bavishi and Rozanski, 2016[24]; Alimujiang et al., 2019[25]), including deaths of despair (Case and Deaton, 2021[26]), but also educational and labour market achievement (Clark, 2001[27]; Clark, Georgellis and Sanfey, 1999[28]; Graham and Pinto, 2021[29]; Martikainen et al., 2022[30]; O'Connor, 2020[31]) and voting behaviours (Algan, Blanc and Senik, 2025[32]; Ward et al., 2021[33]; Ward, 2019[34]). For policy makers concerned about providing cost-effective services to their constituents, and to be able to do so in a sustainable and long-term way, subjective well-being data provide an insight into risks and opportunities for the future health and financial well-being of their population (Blanchflower and Oswald, 2020[35]; Kim, Strecher and Ryff, 2014[36]).
- *To support policy design and evaluation.* Over half of OECD member states have integrated subjective well-being measures into their national well-being initiatives, which in turn have been used to inform strategic planning and performance frameworks, shape new institutional structures and serve as an input to budgeting processes (including as a way of assessing budget proposals on a broader range of outcomes) (OECD, 2023[37]; Durand and Exton, 2019[38]; Exton and Shinwell, 2018[39]). Subjective well-being data have also been used to supplement cost-benefit (CBA) and cost-effectiveness (CEA) analyses, when both designing and evaluating policies (HM Treasury, 2021[40]; Wright, Peasgood and MacLennan, 2017[41]; Clark et al., 2019[42]; Murtin et al., 2017[43]). Guidelines on the use of subjective well-being data have also been issued for businesses, charities and social enterprises interested in measuring the broader impacts of their programmes (Hey, 2018[44]; Measure Wellbeing, 2018[45]; Siegerink and Murtin, 2024[46]).

Updates to OECD recommendations for subjective well-being measurement

The process of updating the *OECD Guidelines on Measuring Subjective Well-being* began in 2023, ten years following the publication of the first edition, with a scoping exercise designed to understand the extent to which those recommendations had been adopted by official data producers in OECD countries. The goal was to understand where measurement recommendations had been accepted and implemented, and where additional guidance from the OECD could be helpful in improving the take-up, usefulness and policy relevance of selected measures. Furthermore, the decade since the publication of the first edition of the *Guidelines* saw a large increase in the number of academic publications centred on subjective well-being data – covering the methods for measuring subjective well-being, its drivers, and its impact on a variety of other well-being outcomes, with implications for policy. The resulting working paper found that country practices had converged around a standardised measure of life satisfaction, but differences persisted in the measures used to capture affect and in the constructs measured to assess eudaimonia (Mahoney, 2023[5]). In reviewing advances in the literature, the same paper also sought both to ensure that the methodological guidance in the first edition remained robust and to understand whether new research had identified conceptual gaps or areas where international guidance could be strengthened.

The working paper set out a streamlined set of research objectives for the updated guidelines:

1. Refine measurement of affect and clarify its relationship to population mental health measures.
2. Seek a clearer definition of, and more meaningful measures for, eudaimonia.
3. Explore more globally inclusive approaches to measurement.
4. Draft measurement recommendations specific to children.

Objectives one through three are covered in this publication and therefore are focused on lessons relevant to surveying adult populations; objective four will be covered in a separate, stand-alone future OECD publication.

To inform the recommendations included in this update, three technical working papers were commissioned from external subject matter experts, to provide an in-depth focus on each of the selected research questions. Each paper conducts a detailed investigation into theoretical frameworks, definitions, and statistical properties and the policy relevance of the target construct. Interested readers can refer to the following supporting documents for more details on each:

- Kudrna, L. et al. (2024[47]), "Measuring affective components of subjective well-being: Updated evidence to inform national data collections", *OECD Papers on Well-being and Inequalities*, No. 31, https://doi.org/10.1787/6c72da70-en.
- Abdallah, S. and J. Mahoney (2024[48]), "Measuring eudaimonic components of subjective well-being: Updated evidence to inform national data collections", *OECD Papers on Well-being and Inequalities*, No. 30, https://doi.org/10.1787/667fbe08-en.
- Smith, C. et al. (2025[49]), "Globally inclusive measures of subjective wellbeing: Updated evidence to inform national data collections", *OECD Papers on Well-being and Inequalities*, No. 35, https://doi.org/10.1787/bd72752a-en.

The findings of these independent research papers provided a starting point for reflecting on the topics addressed by this update, which has also been guided by an informal advisory group (see the Foreword) and further research by the OECD Secretariat, and ultimately by the views expressed by the OECD's Committee on Statistics and Statistical Policy. Annex A provides additional details on procedural matters relating to the update, as well as explanatory information describing how and why measures in Chapters 2 and 3 were selected for inclusion.

Good measurement practice when collecting subjective well-being data

The first edition of the *Guidelines* synthesised evidence from a wide array of sources to summarise the validity and statistical quality of subjective well-being measures, as well as information on how survey design can affect subjective well-being measures – thereby outlining good practice in survey design and methodology. A short summary of the main findings of this analysis are listed below; interested readers can refer to the 2013 *Guidelines* for more detailed discussions and specific references, which remain valid. In particular, Chapter 1 of the 2013 *Guidelines* reviews the reliability and (face, convergent and construct) validity of subjective well-being measures. Chapter 2 overviews question construction; response formats; question context, placement and order effects; mode effects and survey context; and response styles, including cultural contexts. Chapter 3 covers questionnaire design, including suggestions for additional covariates to collect; target population; duration of enumeration; sample size; survey implementation and recommendations for enumerators; and data processing. Finally, Chapter 4 concludes with a discussion on how to report and analyse subjective well-being data (OECD, 2013[1]). While the below sections provide relevant information for subjective well-being data collection in general, Chapters 2 and 3 of this report provide the exact questions and answer scales to use, alongside detailed implementation instructions.

Survey designers should field the questions as they appear, without making changes to the phrasing or the response scale.

Survey vehicles and covariates

To enable the monitoring and benchmarking of societal progress, subjective well-being modules are particularly relevant for household surveys. For example, general social surveys are particularly useful vehicles (Fleischer, Smith and Viac, 2016[50]), since they typically already include a range of other well-being covariates (see the bulleted list below), but subjective well-being measures can also be valuable additions to thematic surveys, while varying the specific modules and measures included depending on the ultimate goal of the corresponding survey: labour force surveys, health surveys, social inclusion surveys, financial inclusion surveys, local area surveys, etc. Time use surveys are well suited to collect data on affect, in particular, since the most accurate affect measures are those that ask respondents to report their experiences over a short (e.g. 24 hour) recall period, and it can be useful to build a picture of how people's affective experiences interact with their time use.

The exact list of covariates that should be measured alongside the subjective well-being module will vary according to the specific needs of the data producers, survey space and the anticipated research question. However, the following is recommended for collection with subjective well-being data in most household surveys:

- *Demographics*: Age, gender, relationship status (legal or social marital status), family composition, number of children, household size, geographic information, migrant status, disability status and – for those data producers already collecting this type of information – data on sexual orientation, race, ethnicity and/or inclusion in a minority group
- *Material conditions:* Household income, consumption, material deprivation, housing quality, employment status
- *Quality of life:* Physical and mental health status (refer to Box 2.7 and Box A A.1 for details on the latter), outcomes related to respondent education and skills, environmental quality and personal security
- *Communal relationships:* Respondent work-life balance and civic engagement and governance, as well as social connections (refer to Box A A.2)

Time use surveys enable data producers to capture fine-grained detail about how people spend their time and with whom. When affect measure(s) are incorporated into time use diaries, it advances an understanding of how people felt while engaging in their activities. In addition to measuring activities (both primary and simultaneous / secondary activities for a given period of time), the following covariates (sometimes referred to as contextual information in time use surveys) should be measured:

- *Time frame:* Time of day and day of the week.
- *Location:* The location of the respondent during each activity (e.g. home, work, school); if the respondent is in transit, the mode of transportation can be specified (e.g. walking, car, bus).
- *With whom*: The other people with the respondent while the activity was ongoing, which advances understanding of the amount of time spent with others vs. spent alone. This question is sometimes divided into two, with the first asking who was with the respondent and the second clarifying who was present, *but not participating* in the activity (UNSD, 2025[51]).

The OECD's Well-being Framework (Box 1.1) provides a useful structure for identifying both some of the key living conditions that shape subjective well-being, as well as some of the life outcomes that evidence increasingly shows may in turn be shaped by subjective well-being. Concurrently, the *OECD Well-being Database* collates internationally comparable data from member states spanning each of the topics listed above; detailed information about the specific measures used to capture information on material conditions, quality of life and communal relationships can be found in the database's metadata document (OECD, 2020[52]).

Target population

The recommendations in this report are designed for the late adolescent and adult population. Many social surveys begin surveying respondents from age 15 or 16 onwards. Specific measurement recommendations for children will be outlined in a forthcoming, companion publication. Regardless of which adult is surveyed in the household, the sampling frame of the survey must ensure a representative sample of individuals can be reported on. Proxy responses – i.e. an individual answering about the subjective well-being of another person in the household – are not appropriate. Subjective well-being data should only be collected directly from individuals themselves.

Frequency and duration of enumeration

The core module of subjective well-being measures (see Box 2.2) should be collected on an annual basis at minimum. If possible, more frequent data collection is recommended. Some OECD national statistical offices have conducted quarterly subjective well-being data collection, which yielded telling insights during the COVID-19 pandemic, the cost of living crisis and in time of geopolitical tensions (OECD, 2021[6]; What Works Wellbeing, 2021[7]; Perona, 2025[8]). Beyond tracking the impact of large shocks, quarterly collection allows subjective well-being data to be reported alongside other quarterly indicators of growth, such as GDP or employment rates (Ametepe et al., 2024[53]).

In an ideal scenario, enumeration of a given survey (i.e. the duration of time the survey is out in the field) would take place over a full year, including all days of the week including holidays. This would remove the biasing effects of seasonality and of certain days of the week, which can influence affect measures in particular due to their shorter recall period ("yesterday" framing, refer to Box 2.5 for more details). However, this is often not feasible for a number of practical reasons. At minimum, enumeration should take place during the same time period each year (to hold seasonal and other effects constant) and be proportionately spread over all days of the week, to the extent possible.

Sample size

Large sample sizes of at least 2 000 respondents (and ideally 5 000 or more) are needed when fielding subjective well-being questions in order to reduce the standard errors of estimates and allow for precise estimates that enable cross-tabulations to analyse and compare outcomes across population sub-groups. Large sample sizes are particularly important for affect modules that use a "yesterday" framing (refer to Box 2.5 for more details). In addition, more heterogenous populations require larger sample sizes to ensure outcomes for population groups can be reliably estimated. Sampling size and methodology should be made available for data users.

Survey mode

The first edition of the *Guidelines* noted that computer-assisted personal interviewing (CAPI) with show cards is considered the ideal mode for collecting data on subjective well-being (show cards that include verbal labels for scale end points are particularly useful when the meaning of the scale and end points change across questions; without show cards, the cognitive burden on respondents can increase). Additionally, some subjective well-being questions touch on sensitive subjects, which means that confidentiality – and ensuring the respondent is in a private space – is important; this can be more difficult to assess when conducting interviews over the phone. However, in the years since the first edition, more national statistical offices have moved to mixed-mode methods for practical (and cost saving) reasons, and the shift to web collection has accelerated in the years since the onset of the COVID-19 pandemic.

Research published in recent years has corroborated findings from the first edition of the *Guidelines* that subjective well-being outcomes are *higher*, on average, for respondents answering over the phone compared to those answering in-person (Dolan and Kavetsos, 2016[54]). However, existing evidence as to the effects of web-based survey modes reveals less definitive conclusions. When comparing web-based to in-person or phone-based surveys, new research shows that responses are consistently *lower* for web-based surveys (Piccitto, Liefbroer and Emery, 2022[55]; Wavrock, Schellenberg and Boulet, 2023[56]), although the magnitude of the differences may not be large, or even statistically significant (Sarracino, Rililo and Mikucka, 2017[57]). On-going investigation into web-based mode effects will help to strengthen and/or corroborate these findings, and provide stronger steers as to good practice moving forward.

Mixed-mode surveys have become more common over the past decade and have since been established as good survey practice – embodying a resource-efficient way to collect household statistics (Eurostat, 2022[58]; Carletto et al., 2022[59]; INSEE, 2022[60]). The COVID-19 pandemic also revealed vulnerabilities in leaning on a single data collection mode (Luiten et al., 2022[61]): for example, data producers relying exclusively on in-person interview methodologies had to quickly create entirely new remote surveying protocols in the face of mandatory social distancing and confinement policies, while those already employing mixed-mode methods could more easily pivot. New publications provide national statistics offices with guidance on how to effectively implement mixed-mode surveys (Schouten et al., 2023[62]).

Whenever possible, national statistical offices and other official data producers are encouraged to collect sufficient information to be able to estimate the impact of mode effects for subjective well-being modules, and the results should be published. The mode used to collect data should always be reported alongside results. When using mixed modes, it is important that questions and response formats are as similar as possible across modes to ensure data comparability. Subjective well-being modules and answer scales in this publication have been designed to work in a variety of formats, including in-person, telephone and web-based surveys.

Question placement

Question placement, and resulting contextual clues, can potentially lead to priming effects that influence responses; for this reason, subjective well-being items should be placed near the start of surveys to minimise these effects. Ideally, the core module (Box 2.2) should be asked immediately following initial screening questions that lead to a respondent's inclusion in the survey. Where this is not practical – for example, if a survey module ordering is not modifiable, or if subjective well-being measures have historically been included as a part of a larger module of other well-being outcomes and data producers do not want to change the ordering for fear of introducing new order effects – then the most vital recommendation is that subjective well-being measures should not immediately follow questions that may elicit strong emotional responses, or that respondents might use to interpret how to respond to subjective well-being questions. Prominent examples include questions about income, political beliefs, employment status, victimisation, discrimination or anything that alludes to social rankings. The best questions to precede subjective well-being modules are relatively neutral demographic questions, such as age, gender or household composition.

Enumerators or survey designers are recommended to use introductory text at the start of the subjective well-being module to distinguish between question topics. This text – whether stated verbally by an enumerator or presented as text in a self-led survey – can serve as a buffer between subjective well-being items and other sensitive questions. Each of the modules in Chapters 2 and 3 contain introductory text.

Question order is also important *within* subjective well-being modules. It is recommended to flow from general to specific questions and to use consistent ordering of individual affect items (alternating between positive and negative items) to reduce the risk that asking either a positive or negative measure first influences subsequent responses. The measures in the recommended modules in Chapters 2 and 3 are designed to be asked in the order in which they appear.

Choice of measures, question wording and answer scales

Question wording matters, and for data to be comparable measures should use standardised phrasing and answer scales. Chapters 2 and 3 provide specific measure recommendations; it is advised to use the exact phrasing and answer formats provided. For data producers currently fielding different iterations of subjective well-being questions, it is recommended that future changes – implemented in order to align with OECD recommendations – be phased in, ideally using parallel split samples, so that the effects of the change can be understood. This will provide data producers with needed information to determine how to address disruptions to the time series and to adjust previous data sets if needed.

For the majority of the subjective well-being questions recommended in these guidelines, the OECD recommends using a 0-to-10 point numerical scale, anchored by verbal labels which represent conceptual absolutes: e.g. *not at all satisfied / completely satisfied*. To obtain more comparable results both between people and in particular across countries, it is advised to label scale interval points – between the anchor points – with numerical (2, 3, 4, etc.), rather than verbal or written (somewhat satisfied, somewhat dissatisfied, etc.) labels, since the latter can prove particularly difficult to translate consistently and may be more susceptible to different interpretations by different people. 0 to 10 numerical scales enable nuanced responses with high analytic value for data users, and (compared to labelled Likert scales) they more strongly prime respondents to consider the scale intervals as equal in size. The order of response categories may be particularly important in the case of phone-based surveys, in which each response category is given a verbal label and no visual aid can be provided. This poses less of a problem for numerical scales – as opposed to Likert scales – and the consistent presentation of the scale from lowest (0) to highest (10) values can reduce respondent burden.

Unipolar scales (containing a continuous scale focused on a single dimension) are recommended for affect measures: for example, anchored by *never/not at all* at one end and *all the time/completely* on the other. Conceptually, it is cleaner to measure affect separately, rather than combining positive and negative affective states into a single bipolar continuum: for example, *very sad* to *very happy*. Data on negative vs. positive affective states should be measured separately, as it is possible for a respondent to report feeling both emotions strongly (or not) over the course of a 24-hour recall period.

The length of the reference period used in subjective well-being questions is particularly critical for measures of affect. When trying to understand affect as it was *experienced*, as opposed to how a respondent feels in *general* (an evaluative measure), or how they remember feeling over a longer period of time (which can be subject to recall bias), reports over a period of 24 hours or less (in the case of time use diaries) are recommended. Conversely, mental health screening tools (see Box 2.7) use a longer reference period – typically the past two, or four weeks. These measures are designed to pick up the *persistent patterns* of affect over a sustained time period, to thereby identify respondents at risk for poor mental health (that is, most everyone experiences momentary feelings of sadness or worry, the signal for poor mental health is very high frequency and/or intensity of such feelings over a prolonged period of time – refer to Box A A.1 for an extended discussion on mental health screening tools vs. affect measures).

Lastly, when cleaning and reporting data from a longer series of items using the same response scale, it is necessary to screen for response sets (when a respondent provides identical responses to a series of items, regardless of the content of the question). These are most visible when the respondent scores at the top or bottom of the scale for all measures (regardless of the measures' direction – e.g. positive or negative valence). Response sets may indicate either a lack of understanding on the part of the respondent, boredom, disengagement or an unwillingness to respond meaningfully. The first best guard against response sets is good survey design, which includes strong consideration for respondent burden and experience as well as keeping batteries of items as short as possible (a practice used consistently throughout the question modules that follow), coupled with transition text that provides a break between items with similar response scales. This procedure cannot correct for the more subtle influences of response sets/social desirability biases, but it can mitigate risks.

Translation

Given the importance of question wording on how people interpret, understand and respond to subjective well-being questions, high quality translations into local languages are critical. Translations should capture the construct the question is designed to measure. A robust translation process, including back translation, is essential. New measures introduced in this edition of the *Guidelines* have, to the extent possible, been tested for translatability and cross-cultural adaptability.

Interviewer training

When subjective well-being data are included in interviewer-led surveys, enumerators should be well-briefed, both on the constructs that the recommended modules aim to capture (so they can answer clarifying questions from respondents) but also on how the collected information will be used and why it is valuable. This enables enumerators to build rapport with interviewees, which diminishes non-response and refusal rates and enhances data quality.

Collecting subjective well-being data in minority populations

The subjective well-being measures and modules included in this publication are designed as far as possible to be relevant to all populations and cultures, across the globe. To further this, in the process of conducting this update and ensuring global inclusivity of the ensuing recommendations, measurement tools and well-being frameworks developed by, or in collaboration with, Indigenous groups and minority communities were reviewed. Indeed, official data producers in many OECD countries have developed well-being surveys tailored to specific communities.

When collecting subjective well-being measures in general, but in particular for minority populations, data producers should be mindful of the following guiding principles (refer to Box A A.3 for an extended discussion of each):

- *Foster community involvement*. Building relationships and trust with the community is important; participatory research methodologies are recommended in that they elevate community voices, priorities and values.
- *Take a strengths-based approach*. There should not be a heavy or unbalanced focus on well-being deprivations or too much emphasis on values that may not be as relevant to the local community (i.e. individual achievement) while devaluing aspects that may be important in other cultural contexts (spirituality, cultural vitality, connection to land). Instead, surveys should seek to find a balance between capturing the resilience, capabilities and assets of communities – as well as vulnerabilities, without too heavy a focus on deficits and problems.
- *Develop local ethical guidelines*. Research practices should be both scientifically sound as well as culturally appropriate and equitable. Attitudes towards privacy, informed consent and the role of community leaders should be tailored to the local context.
- *Ensure data sovereignty*. The local community should govern their data and autonomously make decisions about methods, management and dissemination. Community consultations can help establish these norms.

Reporting central tendency, level and distribution of subjective well-being measures

Summary statistics of central tendency include mean, median and mode: each provides a different and useful way of presenting population averages and comparing levels of subjective well-being across population groups using a single value. Beyond averages, different approaches to reporting the distribution of subjective well-being outcomes highlight inequalities in outcomes across the top and bottom of the distribution and across different population groups. OECD recommendations for reporting the central tendency, level and distribution of subjective well-being data are outlined in Box 1.2.

Box 1.2. Recommended central tendency, level and summary measures of distribution for subjective well-being data

- Use the *mean* to report average levels of subjective well-being. Given the limited number of scale categories (eleven discrete options, when using a 0-10 scale), the median and mode are less sensitive to changes over time or between population groups, in comparison to the mean. When possible, report both the mean as well as the share of the population below a stated threshold. Specific thresholds are described in the implementation details accompanying each module in Chapters 2 and 3; details on thresholds can also be found in the *OECD's Well-being Database* metadata document (OECD, 2020[52]).
- When reporting *deprivations*, it is recommended to check first that the change in the share of the population above and below the threshold paints a consistent picture with that of changes in the distribution as a whole. This is because thresholds can create artificial data cliffs that under- or over-estimate the overall change by focusing on just one cut-point in the distribution. There can also be significant changes in the data on either side of a threshold that are worthy of note, even if the total share of the population above and below a given threshold remains stable.
- Summary measures of distribution (also described as "vertical inequalities") are also of high policy value, and trends in such summary measures should be routinely monitored alongside mean average scores (refer to (OECD, 2017, pp. 68-71[63]) for a detailed discussion of different inequality types and how to measure them in the context of well-being metrics). To provide a summary of the distribution of responses, it is recommended to report the ratio between the top 20% (the quintile with the highest subjective well-being outcomes) and the bottom 20% (the quintile with the lowest). This methodology is used in the *OECD Well-being Database* (OECD, 2020[52]) and in the accompanying *How's Life?* series of publications (OECD, 2024[14]) when reporting on vertical inequalities. To provide a more complete view of the distribution of subjective well-being outcomes, it is also possible to present the share of the population who chose each discrete answer option on the 0 to 10 scale.
- Reporting of "horizontal inequalities", i.e. average results for different population groups, are also of high policy value, especially where time series can illustrate whether gaps in outcomes are narrowing or widening over time. Demographic covariates included in the survey (see above) together with sample sizes will determine the data disaggregations that are possible to report, with age, gender and education breakdowns being a minimum baseline. Additional groups can be considered, should sample sizes permit. Differences in outcomes for vulnerable population groups (including groups at risk of discrimination) can be of particularly high policy relevance. When reporting horizontal inequalities, especially for relatively small populations, care should be taken to assess the statistical significance of differences in outcomes between groups, rather than making simple comparisons between point estimates.

Analysis of subjective well-being data

The first edition of the *Guidelines* contained a full chapter outlining different approaches to analysing subjective well-being data, with different recommendations depending on the ultimate goals of the analytical exercise. Interested readers can refer to Chapter 4 of the 2013 *Guidelines* for a detailed discussion of the following topics:

- Reporting on subjective well-being summary statistics: how to interpret changes over time and differences between population groups, and how to handle cross-country comparisons given concerns around cultural differences in question interpretation and answer patterns.
- How to analyse the drivers and determinants of subjective well-being, and how to manage issues with shared method variance, omitted variables, reverse causality, frame and reference effects, and hedonic adaptation.
- Integrating subjective well-being data into policy processes, including designing, implementing and evaluating policy interventions. Updated examples can also be found in Mahoney (2023[5]).

References

Abdallah, S. and J. Mahoney (2024), "Measuring eudaimonic components of subjective well-being: Updated evidence to inform national data collections", *OECD Papers on Well-being and Inequalities*, No. 30, OECD Publishing, Paris, https://doi.org/10.1787/667fbe08-en. [48]

Algan, Y., C. Blanc and C. Senik (2025), "Trusting others: How unhappiness and social distrust explain populism", in Helliwell, J. et al. (eds.), *The World Happiness Report 2025*, University of Oxford: Wellbeing Research Centre, https://worldhappiness.report/ed/2025/trusting-others-how-unhappiness-and-social-distrust-explain-populism/. [32]

Alimujiang, A. et al. (2019), "Association between life purpose and mortality among US adults older than 50 years", *JAMA Network Open*, Vol. 2/5, https://doi.org/10.1001/JAMANETWORKOPEN.2019.4270. [25]

Ametepe, F. et al. (2024), *PIBien-être 2023 Report*, Institut national de la statistique et des études économiques (STATEC), https://statistiques.public.lu/fr/publications/series/analyses/2024/analyses-01-24.html. [53]

Blanchflower, D. and A. Oswald (2020), "Trends in extreme distress in the United States, 1993–2019", *American Journal of Public Health*, Vol. 110/10, pp. 1538-1544, https://doi.org/10.2105/AJPH.2020.305811. [35]

Carletto, C. et al. (2022), "Positioning household surveys for the next decade", *Statistical Journal of the IAOS*, Vol. 38/3, pp. 923-946, https://content.iospress.com/articles/statistical-journal-of-the-iaos/sji220042. [59]

Case, A. and A. Deaton (2021), "The great divide: Education, despair and death", *NBER Working Papers*, No. 29241, National Bureau of Economic Research, Cambridge, MA, https://doi.org/10.3386/W29241. [26]

Chida, Y. and A. Steptoe (2008), "Positive psychological well-being and mortality: A quantitative review of prospective observational studies", *Psychosomatic Medicine*, Vol. 70/7, pp. 741-756, https://doi.org/10.1097/PSY.0B013E31818105BA. [21]

Clark, A. (2001), "What really matters in a job? Hedonic measurement using quit data", *Labour Economics*, Vol. 8/2, pp. 223-242, https://doi.org/10.1016/S0927-5371(01)00031-8. [27]

Clark, A. et al. (eds.) (2019), *The Origins of Happiness: The Science of Well-being over the Life Course*, Princeton University Press, Princeton, NJ, https://books.google.com/books?hl=en&lr=&id=6ciXDwAAQBAJ&oi=fnd&pg=PP9&dq=the+origins+of+happiness&ots=ZKdX_U8pjm&sig=xRD7b95BcsQkfQfGMsURR2ZQu6Y. [42]

Clark, A., Y. Georgellis and P. Sanfey (1999), "Job satisfaction, wage changes and Quits: Evidence from Germany", SSRN, https://papers.ssrn.com/abstract=132109. [28]

Cohen, R., C. Bavishi and A. Rozanski (2016), "Purpose in life and its relationship to all-cause mortality and cardiovascular events: A meta-analysis", *Psychosomatic Medicine*, Vol. 78/2, pp. 122-133, https://doi.org/10.1097/PSY.0000000000000274. [24]

Cohen, S. et al. (2006), "Positive emotional style predicts resistance to illness after experimental exposure to rhinovirus or influenza a virus", *Psychosomatic Medicine*, Vol. 68/6, pp. 809-815, https://doi.org/10.1097/01.PSY.0000245867.92364.3C. [22]

Delhey, J. and C. Kroll (2012), “Inequality and social integration a 'happiness test' for the new measures of national well-being: How much better than GDP are they?”, *Discussion Papers, Research Unit: Inequality and Social Integration*, Vol. SP I 2012-201, https://ideas.repec.org/p/zbw/wzbisi/spi2012201.html. [15]

Dolan, P. and G. Kavetsos (2016), “Happy talk: Mode of administration effects on subjective well-being”, *Journal of Happiness Studies*, Vol. 17/3, pp. 1273-1291, https://doi.org/10.1007/s10902-015-9642-8. [54]

Durand, M. and C. Exton (2019), “Adopting a well-being approach in central government: Policy mechanisms and practical tools”, in *Global Happiness Policy Report 2019*, Sustainable Development Solutions Network, New York, http://ghwbpr-2019.s3.amazonaws.com/UAE/GH19_Ch8.pdf. [38]

Eurostat (2022), *Position Paper on Mixed-Mode Surveys — 2022 edition*, Publications Office of the European Union, Luxembourg, https://ec.europa.eu/eurostat/fr/web/products-statistical-working-papers/-/ks-tc-21-009. [58]

Exton, C. and M. Shinwell (2018), “Policy use of well-being metrics: Describing countries' experiences”, *OECD Statistics Working Papers*, No. 2018/07, OECD Publishing, Paris, https://doi.org/10.1787/d98eb8ed-en. [39]

Fleischer, L., C. Smith and C. Viac (2016), “A review of general social surveys”, *OECD Statistics Working Papers*, No. 2016/9, OECD Publishing, Paris, https://doi.org/10.1787/bb54d16f-en. [50]

Graham, C. and S. Pinto (2021), “The geography of desperation in America: Labor force participation, mobility, place, and well-being”, *Social Science & Medicine*, Vol. 270, p. 113612, https://doi.org/10.1016/J.SOCSCIMED.2020.113612. [29]

Graham, C. and S. Pinto (2019), “Unequal hopes and lives in the USA: Optimism, race, place, and premature mortality”, *Journal of Population Economics*, Vol. 32/2, pp. 665-733, https://www.jstor.org/stable/48699052. [23]

Hadzi-Vaskov, M. and L. Ricci (2021), “Understanding Chile's social unrest in an international perspective”, *IMF Working Paper*, No. 21/174, International Monetary Fund, https://www.imf.org/en/Publications/WP/Issues/2021/06/25/Understanding-Chiles-Social-Unrest-in-an-International-Perspective-461279. [17]

Hey, N. (2018), *Improve wellbeing with data infrastructure: Seven actions for organisations*, What Works Wellbeing, https://whatworkswellbeing.org/blog/improve-wellbeing-with-data-infrastructure-seven-actions-for-organisations/. [44]

HM Treasury (2021), *Wellbeing Guidance for Appraisal: Supplementary Green Book Guidance*, Social Impacts Task Force, https://www.gov.uk/government/publications/green-book-supplementary-guidance-wellbeing. [40]

Ianchovichina, E. (2018), “Eruptions of Popular Anger: The Economics of the Arab Spring and Its Aftermath”, *MENA Development Report*, World Bank, Washington, DC, https://documents1.worldbank.org/curated/en/251971512654536291/pdf/121942-REVISED-Eruptions-of-Popular-Anger-preliminary-rev.pdf (accessed on 22 March 2023). [16]

INSEE (2022), *Le multimode dans les enquêtes auprès des ménages : une collecte modernisée, un processus complexifié – Courrier des statistiques N7 - 2022*, Institut national de la statistique et des études économiques (INSEE), https://www.insee.fr/fr/information/6035934?sommaire=6035950. [60]

Kaiser, C. and A. Oswald (2022), "The scientific value of numerical measures of human feelings", *PNAS*, Vol. 119/42, https://doi.org/10.1073/pnas.2210412119. [20]

Kim, E., V. Strecher and C. Ryff (2014), "Purpose in life and use of preventive health care services", *Proceedings of the National Academy of Sciences of the United States of America*, Vol. 111/46, pp. 16331-16336, https://doi.org/10.1073/PNAS.1414826111. [36]

Kudrna, L. et al. (2024), "Measuring affective components of subjective well-being: Updated evidence to inform national data collections", *OECD Papers on Well-being and Inequalities*, No. 31, OECD Publishing, Paris, https://doi.org/10.1787/6c72da70-en. [47]

Luiten, A. et al. (2022), *Mixed-Mode Official Surveys: Design and Analysis*, Centraal Bureau voor de Statistiek (CBS), https://unstats.un.org/iswghs/events/mixed-mode-webinar/UN-WG-Household-Surveys-webinar-17-11-22.pdf. [61]

Mahoney, J. (2023), "Subjective well-being measurement: Current practice and new frontiers", *OECD Papers on Well-being and Inequalities*, Vol. 17, https://doi.org/10.1787/4e180f51-en. [5]

Martikainen, S. et al. (2022), "Moments of meaningfulness and meaninglessness: A qualitative inquiry into affective eudaimonia at work", *Article Group & Organization Management*, Vol. 47/6, pp. 1135-1180, https://doi.org/10.1177/10596011211047324. [30]

Measure Wellbeing (2018), *Evaluating Wellbeing – Better Evaluations for Social Change*, Nottingham Trent University, https://measure-wellbeing.org/. [45]

Morozink, J. et al. (2025), "Educational disparities in 20-year trajectories of psychological well-being in a national sample", *Scientific Reports*, Vol. 15/1, pp. 1-12, https://doi.org/10.1038/s41598-025-95058-y. [19]

Murtin, F. et al. (2017), "Beyond GDP: Is there a law of one shadow price?", *European Economic Review*, Vol. 100, pp. 390-411, https://doi.org/10.1016/J.EUROECOREV.2017.09.001. [43]

O'Connor, K. (2020), "Life satisfaction and noncognitive skills: Effects on the likelihood of unemployment", *Kyklos*, Vol. 73/4, pp. 568-604, https://doi.org/10.1111/KYKL.12226. [31]

OECD (2024), *How's Life? 2024: Well-being and Resilience in Times of Crisis*, OECD Publishing, Paris, https://doi.org/10.1787/90ba854a-en. [14]

OECD (2023), *Economic Policy Making to Pursue Economic Welfare: Report Prepared for the 2023 Japan Presidency of the G7*, OECD Publishing, Paris, https://www.oecd.org/economy/G7_Beyond_GDP_Economic_policy_making_to_pursue_economic_welfare_2023.pdf. [37]

OECD (2023), *Measuring Population Mental Health*, OECD Publishing, Paris, https://doi.org/10.1787/5171eef8-en. [13]

OECD (2021), *COVID-19 and Well-being: Life in the Pandemic*, OECD Publishing, Paris, https://doi.org/10.1787/1e1ecb53-en. [6]

OECD (2020), *How's Life? 2020: Measuring Well-being*, OECD Publishing, Paris, https://doi.org/10.1787/9870c393-en. [52]

OECD (2017), *How's Life? 2017: Measuring Well-being*, OECD Publishing, Paris, https://doi.org/10.1787/how_life-2017-en. [63]

OECD (2017), *OECD Guidelines on Measuring the Quality of the Working Environment*, OECD Publishing, Paris, https://doi.org/10.1787/9789264278240-en. [12]

OECD (2017), *OECD Guidelines on Measuring Trust*, OECD Publishing, Paris, https://doi.org/10.1787/9789264278219-en. [11]

OECD (2013), *OECD Framework for Statistics on the Distribution of Household Income, Consumption and Wealth*, OECD Publishing, Paris, https://doi.org/10.1787/9789264194830-en. [10]

OECD (2013), *OECD Guidelines for Micro Statistics on Household Wealth*, OECD Publishing, Paris, https://doi.org/10.1787/9789264194878-en. [9]

OECD (2013), *OECD Guidelines on Measuring Subjective Well-being*, OECD Publishing, Paris, https://doi.org/10.1787/9789264191655-en. [1]

OECD (2011), *How's Life?: Measuring Well-being*, OECD Publishing, Paris, https://doi.org/10.1787/9789264121164-en. [2]

Perona, M. (2025), *Le Bien-être des Français, Mars 2025*, CEntre Pour la Recherche EconoMique et ses APplications (CEPREMAP), https://www.cepremap.fr/2025/04/le-bien-etre-des-francais-mars-2025/. [8]

Piccitto, G., A. Liefbroer and T. Emery (2022), "Does the survey mode affect the association between subjective well-being and its determinants? An experimental comparison between face-to-face and web mode", *Journal of Happiness Studies*, Vol. 23/7, pp. 3441-3461, https://doi.org/10.1007/S10902-022-00553-Y. [55]

Ryff, C. (2024), "The privilege of well-being in an increasingly unequal society", *Current Directions in Psychological Science*, https://doi.org/10.1177/09637214241266818. [18]

Sarracino, F., C. Rililo and M. Mikucka (2017), "Comparability of web and telephone survey modes for the measurement of subjective well-being", *Survey Research Methods : SRM*, Vol. 11/2, pp. 141-169, https://madoc.bib.uni-mannheim.de/43970/. [57]

Schouten, B. et al. (2023), *Mixed-mode official surveys: Design and analysis*, Chapman & Hall, https://www.routledge.com/Mixed-Mode-Official-Surveys-Design-and-Analysis/Schouten-vandenBrakel-Buelens-Giesen-Luiten-Meertens/p/book/9781032102962. [62]

Siegerink, V. and F. Murtin (2024), "An OECD survey of employee well-being: An instrument to measure employee well-being inside companies", *OECD Papers on Well-being and Inequalities*, No. 24, OECD Publishing, Paris, https://doi.org/10.1787/74f48e24-en. [46]

Smith, C. et al. (2025), "Globally inclusive measures of subjective well-being: Updated evidence to inform national data collections", *OECD Papers on Well-being and Inequalities*, No. 35, OECD Publishing, Paris, https://doi.org/10.1787/bd72752a-en. [49]

Stiglitz, J., J. Fitoussi and M. Durand (eds.) (2018), *For Good Measure: Advancing Research on Well-being Metrics Beyond GDP*, OECD Publishing, Paris, https://doi.org/10.1787/9789264307278-en. [4]

Stiglitz, J., A. Sen and J. Fitoussi (2009), *Report by the Commission on the Measurement of Economic Performance and Social Progress*, https://ec.europa.eu/eurostat/documents/8131721/8131772/Stiglitz-Sen-Fitoussi-Commission-report.pdf. [3]

UNSD (2025), *Guide to Producing Statistics on Time Use*, United Nations Statistics Division, https://unstats.un.org/UNSDWebsite/statcom/session_55/documents/BG-3k-Guide_to_Producing_Statistics_on_Time_Use-55UNSC_background-E.pdf. [51]

Ward, G. (2019), "Happiness and voting behavior", in Helliwell, J., R. Layard and J. Sachs (eds.), *World Happiness Report 2019*, Sustainable Development Solutions Network, New York, https://worldhappiness.report/ed/2019/happiness-and-voting-behavior/. [34]

Ward, G. et al. (2021), "(Un)happiness and voting in U.S. presidential elections", *Journal of Personality and Social Psychology*, Vol. 120/2, pp. 370-383, https://doi.org/10.1037/PSPI0000249. [33]

Wavrock, D., G. Schellenberg and C. Boulet (2023), *Survey Framing and Mode Effects in Life Satisfaction Responses on Canadian Social Surveys*, Statistics Canada, https://www150.statcan.gc.ca/n1/pub/36-28-0001/2023001/article/00003-eng.htm. [56]

What Works Wellbeing (2021), *What helped the UK cope with the Covid-19 pandemic and lockdowns?*, What Works Wellbeing Centre, https://whatworkswellbeing.org/resources/what-helped-the-uk-cope-with-the-covid-19-pandemic-and-lockdowns/ (accessed on 15 April 2025). [7]

Wright, L., T. Peasgood and S. MacLennan (2017), *A Guide to Wellbeing Economic Evaluation*, What Works Wellbeing Centre, https://whatworkswellbeing.org/resources/a-guide-to-wellbeing-economic-evaluation/. [41]

2. Core and extended survey modules

This chapter contains recommended subjective well-being modules to be integrated into official surveys. These include (1) a core module, which contains a concise set of measures that span the different components of subjective well-being (life evaluation, affect and eudaimonia), each with strong statistical properties and unique predictive power for policy-relevant outcomes; (2) extended modules for each component area, alongside a module for population mental health measures, and (3) a discussion of time use survey integration. Implementation instructions for each module are also provided. The modules are designed to be ready-for-use in official surveys, due to their brevity and explicit accompanying instructions on question phrasing, response scales and implementation details.

This chapter presents a series of short subjective well-being modules that can be integrated into existing surveys. Each module is accompanied by a brief description of the measures contained therein, along with instructions for how to implement and (where relevant) how to interpret the resulting data. The following modules are included in this chapter: a core module of subjective well-being (Box 2.2); extended modules for life evaluation (Box 2.3), domain evaluation (Box 2.4), affect (Box 2.5), eudaimonia (Box 2.6) and population mental health (Box 2.7); and a discussion of time use survey modules (Box 2.8).

The purpose of creating a *core module* of subjective well-being measures is to provide official data producers with a short set of the strongest-performing measures, in terms of a range of selection criteria including statistical quality and policy relevance (Box 2.1). Adding questions to official surveys is resource intensive: fielding new questions requires time and additional expense and can contribute to respondent fatigue. The brevity of the core module enables data producers to incorporate a set of subjective well-being questions that span evaluative, affective and eudaimonic concepts into different types of household surveys, including general social surveys, community health surveys, and specialised surveys on specific topics such as social cohesion or trust, etc. The short nature of the module also enables it to be fielded more frequently (ideally at least annually).

For survey designers with sufficient resources and an interest in collecting more detailed subjective well-being data, more flexible *extended modules* for each dimension of subjective well-being are provided. The extended modules identify important conceptual areas to measure and, for each, select one measure that the evidence shows is most valid for measurement. Each module also identifies a priority short list of measures as well as additional extended options. Items in the extended modules that also appear in the core module are in **bold**.

Box 2.1. Measure selection criteria

Four criteria govern how measures are selected into the modules. These criteria are applied to the core as well as extended modules; however, they are applied more strictly to the core.

- *Statistical properties*: Measures need to have strong evidence for their psychometric properties, including statistical validity and reliability, across population groups.
- *Brevity*: Measures for a given concept should be concise and, ideally, single-item questions.
- *Unique policy relevance*: Selected measures should be meaningful for policy-relevant outcomes – including, but not limited to, physical and mental health, financial, labour market, relational and civic engagement outcomes – justifying their inclusion in large-scale official data collections. Importantly, a measure should reflect meaningful outcomes for *all* populations, globally, to the degree that this is possible. Of particular consideration for the core module: measures should have unique and complementary value-add compared to others in the set, demonstrating the need to include all items.
- *Consistency*: There is significant value in having generally agreed-upon statistical standards and potential harm in changing existing standards and disrupting long-running time series. When new measures are considered, consistency with other OECD measurement recommendations, as well as with existing national or international data collection practices, is prioritised.

Annex A provides detailed explanations for the decisions underpinning which concepts and measures to include in each of the modules.

Data producers may approach subjective well-being measurement from different starting points. For those who are not currently measuring subjective well-being, it is recommended to begin with the core module. Where survey space allows, those looking for a more in-depth understanding of the different components of subjective well-being can expand their efforts by including priority measures from the extended modules. Data producers particularly interested in increasing the global inclusivity of their measures may wish to explore the *cross-cutting* experimental module and question banks provided in Chapter 3. Figure 2.1 provides data producers with a flowchart of the modules contained in these guidelines to aid in their selection of subjective well-being measures for household (Panel A) and time use (Panel B) surveys.

Figure 2.1. A flowchart to guide subjective well-being module selection

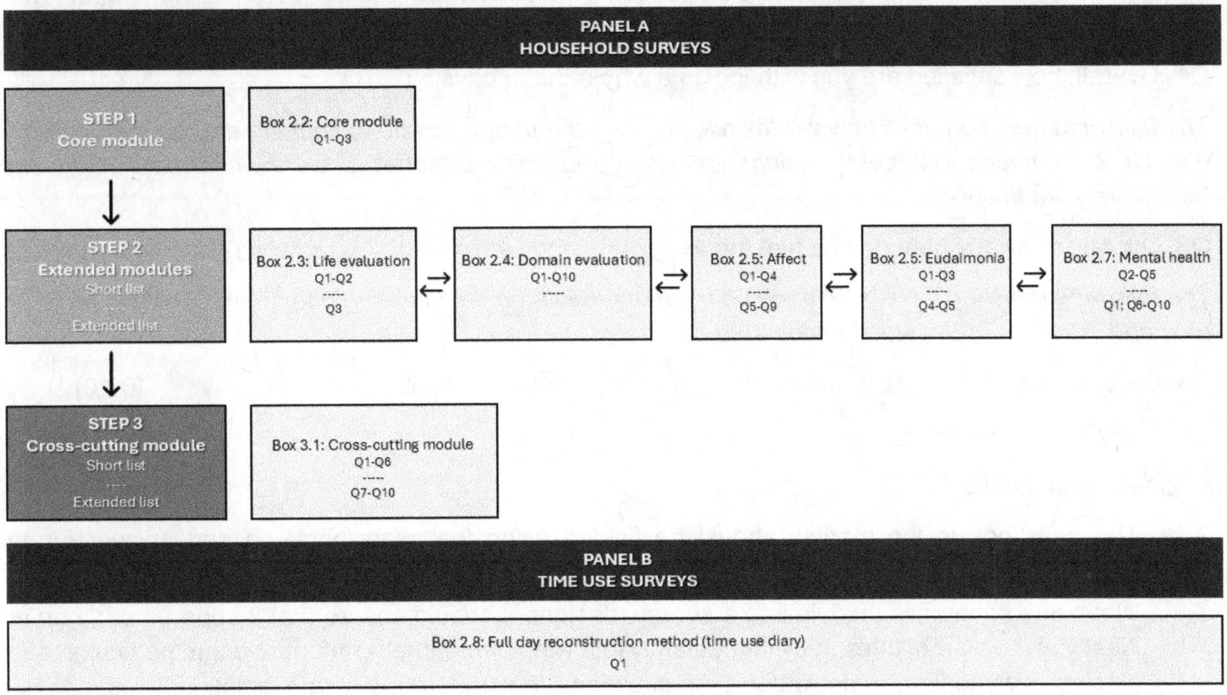

Note: Panel A: Steps appear in order of priority. Data producers interested in fielding subjective well-being questions in household surveys should begin with the core module (Step 1); following this, if desired, data producers can include priority measures from the extended modules (Step 2), which are not presented in any order of importance given that all provide added value; for data producers with sufficient space and interest, the cross-cutting module (Step 3) can then also be used. The extended modules and cross-cutting module contain a short list of measures, as well as an extended list of measures should space allow. Modules in Step 1 and Step 2 appear in this chapter; the module in Step 3 appears in Chapter 3. Panel B: One time use module is recommended and appears in this chapter; the Annex provides details on alternate approaches, depending on the structure of the survey, technical resources and availability of space.

A core module for measuring subjective well-being in household surveys

The core module contains three measures, with a single question for each of the subjective well-being components: a summary measure for life evaluation (Q1) and for eudaimonia (Q2) and one example measure of affect (Q3) (Box 2.2). The measures included have the strongest evidence for their validity, relevance and international comparability (refer to Annex A).

Box 2.2. Core module of subjective well-being measures

The following question asks how satisfied you feel, on a scale from 0 to 10. Zero means you feel "not at all satisfied" and 10 means you feel "completely satisfied".

Q1. Overall, how satisfied are you with life as a whole these days? [0-10]

The following question asks how worthwhile you feel the things you do in your life are, on a scale from 0 to 10. Zero means you feel the things you do in your life are "not at all worthwhile", and 10 means "completely worthwhile".

Q2. Overall, to what extent do you feel the things you do in your life are worthwhile? [0-10]

The following question asks how much pain you have felt, on a scale from 0 to 10, where 0 refers to no pain and 10 refers to the worst imaginable pain.

Q3. Over the past 7 days, how would you rate your pain on average? [0-10]

Implementation details:

- The questions in the module should be fielded using the exact phrasing and answer formats provided. Questions should be asked in the order in which they appear.
- When integrating this module into a survey, designers should ensure that it appears early on and ideally at the start of the survey immediately following demographic information. In particular, avoid placing this module immediately after questions that may elicit strong emotional responses in respondents or questions that may frame how respondents interpret this module (e.g. items on health or household finances).
- Q1, an evaluative question asking respondents how satisfied they are with their life, is the *primary measure* of subjective well-being. If space only allows for a single item, it should be Q1.
- For data producers already capturing a measure of pain in separate surveys (most often health surveys), it is still recommended to collect Q3, in particular if the other measure of pain focuses on "physical" or "bodily" pain, or assesses the functional limitation pain plays in performing daily activities. These questions are important in their own right but capture different information and have different policy applications. For a longer discussion on this, refer to Annex A. For a precise definition of pain, refer to the "Guidelines for interviewers" section below, as well as Annex A.

Origin:

- Both Q1 and Q2 appear in the original 2013 OECD Guidelines on Measuring Subjective Well-being.
- Q3 is a form of the Numerical Pain Rating Scale (NPRS), a single-item pain assessment tool that has been validated in clinical settings. This question appears in the PROMIS (patient-reported outcomes measurement information system) Adult Short Form survey and is also included in the OECD's Patient Reported Indicator Survey (PaRIS) (refer to Annex A for details).

Time:

- The module is expected to take about 60 seconds to complete.

Output:

- Data on life satisfaction (Q1) and feelings about things in life being worthwhile (Q2) can be presented as the mean value of responses, excluding missing values. Summary measures of distribution (inequalities), such as the standard deviation of responses and the ratio of the top 20% of outcomes compared to the bottom 20%, should be reported (refer to Box 1.2 for details). The mean value and standard error of this estimate can be used to describe differences in outcomes between different population groups.
- The percentage of the population reporting an outcome below a threshold (a score ≤ 4) should also be reported to identify those with "low life satisfaction" and those who feel that the things they do in in life are "not worthwhile".
- Data on pain (Q3) can be presented as the mean value of responses, excluding missing values, as for Q1 and Q2. In addition, the percentage of the population reporting "no pain" (a score of 0) or "mild" (a score ≥ 1 and ≤ 4), "moderate" (5-6) or "severe" (a score ≥ 7) pain can also be reported.

Guidelines for interviewers:

- The primary question (Q1) deliberately focuses on how people are feeling "these days" rather than specifying a longer or shorter time period. The intent is not to obtain the current emotional state of the respondent, but to obtain a cognitive evaluation on their level of life satisfaction.
- The eudaimonic question (Q2) concerns the extent to which people feel their activities in general ("the things you do in your life") are worthwhile, in the sense that their activities contribute to attaining personally valued goals. If the concept of "worthwhile" is difficult to translate to the local language, translators should be advised that the question gets at the underlying construct of one's life having a sense of meaning or purpose. The question is *not* intended to ask respondents whether they feel their life is worth living, and translations should take care to make this distinction. What is deemed meaningful and worthwhile is determined by the respondent; the question should not be asked in a context that could prompt respondents to think about achievements in particular domains of life (such as work). No specific time frame is supplied: respondents are invited to make an overall assessment.
- The question on pain (Q3) refers to pain in general and makes no distinction between physical and psychological pain given there is reasonable consensus in the medical and psychological literatures advising against such a strict delineation and noting that pain by definition contains an emotional component (see Annex A for an extended discussion). The International Association for the Study of Pain defines pain as "An unpleasant sensory and emotional experience associated with, or resembling that associated with, actual or potential tissue damage" that "is always a personal experience that is influenced to varying degrees by biological, psychological and social factors" (Raja et al., 2020[1]). This definition can be used as a reference when translating this question to local languages, in particular if the word "pain" in the target language typically is associated only with physical pain. Enumerators can also use this definition to help prompt respondents if they express confusion as to the target construct of the question.

Extended modules for subjective well-being concepts

The following modules provide additional measurement recommendations for each component of subjective well-being. It is recommended that extended modules are fielded as a second-order priority, after the core module has been implemented in full. Whenever an item in an extended module also appears in the core module, it appears in bold and should be asked only once per survey.

When cleaning and reporting data from a longer series of items using the same response scale, it is recommended to screen for potential response sets. These can be visible when the respondent scores at the top or bottom of the scale for all indicators (regardless of the indicators' direction – e.g. positive or negative valence). Response sets may indicate either a lack of understanding on the part of the respondent, boredom, disengagement or an unwillingness to respond meaningfully. The first best guard against response sets is to mitigate their risk through good survey design, and all of the modules included here are designed to keep the battery of items as short as possible, coupled with transition text that provides a break between items with similar response scales.

Life evaluation

There are two extended modules under the life evaluation heading – the first is an extended module for general assessments of life evaluation, which focus on life in general, or life overall. The second is a domain evaluation extended module, which asks respondents to reflect on their satisfaction with specific aspects of their lives.

The life evaluation extended module contains questions regarding a respondent's cognitive judgements on how they evaluate their own lives (Box 2.3). The bolded question (Q1) also appears in the core module. Q2 captures information on a respondent's perception of their life satisfaction in the past, and Q3 provides insight into a respondent's perceptions of the future.

Box 2.3. Life evaluation extended module

The following two questions ask how satisfied you feel, on a scale from 0 to 10. Zero means you feel "not at all satisfied" and 10 means you feel "completely satisfied".

Q1. Overall, how satisfied are you with life as a whole these days? [0-10]

Q2. Overall, how satisfied with your life were you one year ago? [0-10]

Q3. Overall, how hopeful do you feel about your future, where 0 is "not at all hopeful", and 10 is "completely hopeful"? [0-10]

Implementation details:

- The questions in the module should be fielded using the exact phrasing and answer formats provided. Questions are designed be used as a set and asked in the order in which they appear. Where space limitations prevent adoption of the full module, Q2 can be prioritised over Q3. (Q1 is the primary measure of the core module and should always have priority over other measures.)
- Q3 is a new question for this edition of the *Guidelines*; refer to Annex A for more details on its statistical properties and the policy relevance of hope.

Time:

- The module is expected to take about 60 seconds to complete in its entirety.

Origin:

- Q1 appears in the core module and also appeared in the original 2013 *OECD Guidelines on Measuring Subjective Well-being*.
- An earlier version of Q2, with a 5-year rather than 1-year recall period, appeared in the original *OECD Guidelines* (see Annex A for more on the rationale for this change).
- Q3 was introduced by the Office for National Statistics in the United Kingdom in 2023 (ONS, 2024[2]).

Output:

- All indicators can be presented as the mean value of responses, excluding missing values. Summary measures of distribution (inequalities) should also be reported (see Box 1.2 for details). The mean value and standard error can be used to describe differences in outcomes between different population groups.
- The percentage of the population reporting an outcome below a threshold (a score ≤ 4) should also be reported in order to identify those with "low life satisfaction" now (Q1) and one year ago (Q2) and those who feel "little hope" for their future (Q3).

Guidelines for interviewers:

- These questions deliberately focus on how people are feeling about life as a whole rather than specifying a longer or shorter time period, and they ask the respondents for a reflective judgement rather than a statement of their current mood.
- The question on hope (Q3) refers to both respondents' positive outlook towards the future as well as their sense that they have the ability (or agency) to achieve good outcomes, which can be prompted if there is confusion on the respondent's side. The word "hope" is used in English to distinguish from optimism, which is more associated with stable personality traits. However, this distinction may not translate across languages; in some languages, the word "optimism" may be a better fit to capture the intended meaning.

Domain evaluations collect respondents' evaluative judgements on how well different specific aspects of their lives are going (Box 2.4), using the same framing as the satisfaction with life question included in the core module and the life evaluation extended module. The questions in the module capture people's satisfaction with various domains of life but are distinct from self-reported measures of outcomes in these domains given the focus on *satisfaction* over self-assessment (e.g. satisfaction with health status vs. self-reported good vs. poor health). Domain evaluations can help to pinpoint particular areas of (dis)satisfaction in people's lives and have in some cases been associated with behaviour (Kaiser and Oswald, 2022[3]): job dissatisfaction predicts job quits (Clark, 2001[4]; Clark, Georgellis and Sanfey, 1999[5]) and marital dissatisfaction predicts divorce (Powdthavee, 2009[6]), for example.

Box 2.4. Domain evaluation extended module

The following questions ask how satisfied you feel about specific aspects of your life, on a scale from 0 to 10. Zero means you feel "not at all satisfied" and 10 means you feel "completely satisfied".

Q1. How satisfied are you with your standard of living?	[0-10]
Q2. How satisfied are you with your health?	[0-10]
Q3. How satisfied are you with what you are achieving in life?	[0-10]
Q4. How satisfied are you with your personal relationships?	[0-10]
Q5. How satisfied are you with how safe you feel?	[0-10]
Q6. How satisfied are you with feeling part of your community?	[0-10]
Q7. How satisfied are you with your future security?	[0-10]
Q8. How satisfied are you with the amount of time you have to do the things that you like doing?	[0-10]
Q9. How satisfied are you with the quality of your local environment?	[0-10]
Only for respondents who are employed:	
Q10. How satisfied are you with your job?	[0-10]

Implementation details:

- The questions in the module should be fielded using the exact phrasing and answer formats provided. Questions are designed to be used as a set and asked in the order in which they appear.
- Since the questions in the module cover evaluative forms of subjective well-being, they can be asked immediately following questions in the life evaluation extended module (Box 2.3).

Time:

- This module takes about 3 minutes to complete in its entirety.

Origin:

- The full module appeared in the original 2013 OECD Guidelines on Measuring Subjective Well-being.
- Questions 1-7 refer to items in the Personal Wellbeing Index (PWI) (International Wellbeing Group, 2024[7]).

Output:

- Information on individual questions can be presented as the mean value of each response, omitting missing values. Summary measures of distribution (inequalities) should also be reported (see Box 1.2 for details). The mean value of responses, and the standard error of this estimate, can be used to describe differences between population groups.
- The percentage of the population reporting scores below a "low satisfaction" threshold (a score ≤ 4) should also be reported.

Guidelines for interviewers:

- Respondents are asked to evaluate their satisfaction with various domains of their life; each domain should be considered separately.

Affect

Affect refers to a person's feelings or emotional states, measured with respect to a specific period of time. This module collects information on positive and negative emotional states experienced the day before the survey (Box 2.5). (Refer to Box A A.1 in the Annex for a discussion of the difference between affect and mental health measures and the policy applications of both.)

Box 2.5. Affect extended module

The following questions ask about how you felt yesterday on a scale from 0 to 10. Zero means you did not experience the feeling "at all" yesterday while 10 means you experienced the feeling "all of the time" yesterday. Here is a list of ways you might have felt yesterday.

Q1. How about happy?	[0-10]
Q2. How about worried?	[0-10]
Q3. How about calm?	[0-10]
Q4. How about sad?	[0-10]

Q5. How about angry?	[0-10]
Q6. How about joyful?	[0-10]
Q7. How about tired?	[0-10]
Q8. How about stressed?	[0-10]
Q9. Did you smile or laugh a lot yesterday?	[0-10]

Implementation details:

- This module is designed for use in very large sample surveys only, so that the aggregate of experiences "yesterday" sum to a population-representative picture of affect, regardless of how (a)typical yesterday was for each individual respondent. It is not suitable for surveys of fewer than 2 000 respondents (and ideally should have a minimum of 5 000 respondents).
- The questions in the module should be fielded using the exact phrasing and answer formats provided. Questions are designed be used as a set and asked in the order in which they appear. In case of limited space, only Q1-4 should be asked.
- Q1, Q3, Q6 and Q9 capture aspects of positive affect; Q2, Q4, Q5, Q7 and Q8 capture aspects of negative affect. There are more negative than positive questions, reflecting evidence that negative affect is more multidimensional than positive affect (see Annex A).
- Q1, Q2, Q5, Q6, Q8 and Q9 are measures of high arousal, while Q3, Q4 and Q7 are measures of low arousal.
- Interested survey designers with sufficient space may be interested in supplementing this module with affect measures from the cross-cutting experimental module (see Box 3.1).

Time:

- This module is expected to take about 3 minutes to complete in its entirety.

Origin:

- Q1-5 and Q7-9 appeared in the original OECD *Guidelines*. Q3 was developed by the Gallup-WPE Global Wellbeing Initiative and continues to be fielded in Gallup's annual World Poll (Lambert et al., 2020[8]).
- Q6 has been slightly adapted from the original *OECD Guidelines*, changing "enjoyment" to "joyful" (see Annex A for the rationale).

Output:

- It is recommended to present the answers to individual questions to provide information on particular emotional states.
  - Information on individual questions can be presented as the mean value of each response, omitting missing values. Summary measures of distribution (inequalities) should also be reported (see Box 1.2 for details). The mean value of responses, and the standard error of this estimate, can be used to describe differences between population groups.
  - For each individual question, the percentage of the population reporting a score exceeding a certain threshold (a score ≤ 4 for positive affect and a score ≥ 6 for negative affect) should also be reported: this designates the share of the population with "low levels" of each positive emotion or with "high levels" of each negative emotion on the day prior.
- In addition to reporting outcomes for individual questions, it is also possible to calculate a composite measure of balance between positive and negative affects, which enables comparison across countries in that affect balance calculations smooth out cultural and regional differences in the propensity to report extreme emotions (both positive and negative).
  - A composite measure of positive affect can be calculated as the mean score for Q1, Q3, Q6 and Q9.
  - A composite measure of negative affect can be calculated as the mean score for Q2, Q4, Q5, Q7 and Q8.
  - Affect balance is then calculated as positive affect minus negative affect for each respondent, averaged across all respondents. This will give a value ranging from -10 to +10. It is recommended to report the share of the population with a negative affect balance (a score less than 0).
  - Note that if this module is implemented alongside the core module (Box 2.2), it is *not* recommended that the pain measure from the core module (Q3) be included in the affect balance calculation; the pain measure uses an *intensity* rather than a *frequency* framing; it uses a different labelling scheme for the response scale; and it uses a different recall period (past seven days), making the question less comparable to the set of affect questions in this module.

Guidelines for interviewers:

- The aim of the module is to capture information on respondents' feelings, states, moods or emotions on the previous day. The time frame is explicitly short, because the primary focus is the affective states that people actually experienced, which is most accurately recalled over short time periods. If a respondent indicates that the previous day was unusual in some respect (something particularly bad or good happened, or they were feeling unwell), they should still report how they felt that day, since this question is intended to capture the feelings that people have actually experienced, not how people feel on a "typical" day. These affect items are designed to be used in very large sample household surveys only: under these conditions, because several thousand people should be interviewed over a relatively long period of time over the course of a household survey, unusual events will not overly bias the aggregated statistics that are produced. More importantly, the reference to a specific day permits the data to be used to unravel day-of-week effects and responses to external events for which the dates are known.

Eudaimonia

Eudaimonia is broadly defined as a feeling that one is living well, encompassing a sense of meaning, purpose and autonomy in life, together with self-acceptance, feelings of competence, and personal growth. The questions in this module are designed to capture important constructs of eudaimonia, including: a sense that the things one does in life have worth, meaning and purpose (Q1); a sense of autonomy (Q2); a feeling of competence, accomplishment or environmental mastery (Q3); self-esteem or self-acceptance (Q4); and personal growth (Q5) (Box 2.6). (Relatedness, another construct of eudaimonia, is not included in this module given that it is collected as a part of social connections measurement efforts – refer to Box A A.2. for a discussion on this.)

Box 2.6. Eudaimonia extended module

The following question asks how worthwhile you feel the things you do in your life are, on a scale from 0 to 10. Zero means you feel the things you do in your life are "not at all worthwhile", and 10 means you feel they are "completely worthwhile".

Q1. Overall, to what extent do you feel the things you do in your life are worthwhile? [0-10]

For the following questions, please use a scale from 0 to 10 to indicate how you feel. Zero means you "disagree completely" and 10 means you "agree completely".

Q2. I am able to do things that I really want and value in life. [0-10]

Q3. Most days I get a sense of accomplishment from what I do. [0-10]

Q4. In general, I feel very positive about myself. [0-10]

Q5. For me, life has been a continuous process of learning, changing and growth. [0-10]

Implementation details:

- The questions in the module should be fielded using the exact phrasing and answer formats provided. Questions are designed to be used as a set and asked in the order in which they appear.
- Given limited space, only Q1-Q3 can be implemented.
- Q5 is a new measure; refer to Annex A for more details on its statistical properties and the policy relevance of a sense of personal growth.

Time:

- This module is expected to take about 3 minutes to complete in its entirety.

Origin:

- Q1 appears in the core module and appeared in the original *OECD Guidelines,* as did Q3-4.

- Q2 has been used in the Finnish Citizen's Pulse Survey led by the Prime Minister's Office (Statistics Finland, 2024[9]), and it will also be included in the 2025 European Social Survey (Rutherford et al., 2024[10]). It has been adapted to use a 0-10 answer scale.
- Q5 is a single item in the Shortened Psychological Wellbeing Scale (Ryff and Keyes, 1995[11]), and it too has been adapted to use a 0-10 answer scale.

Output:

- Information on individual questions can be presented as the mean value of each response, omitting missing values. Summary measures of distribution (inequalities) should also be reported (see Box 1.2 for details). The mean value of responses, and the standard error of this estimate, can be used to describe differences between population groups.
- The percentage of the population reporting scores below a threshold (a score ≤ 4) can also be reported.

Guidelines for interviewers:

- The questions in this module assess the degree to which respondents agree or disagree with various statements about themselves. They are intended to capture how people see themselves rather than emotions or feelings they have experienced. As a result, the questions are about how people are now and do not refer to a specific time period.

Population mental health

Mental health is defined by the World Health Organization as "a state of mental well-being that enables people to cope with the stresses of life, realise their abilities, learn well and work well, and contribute to their community" (WHO, 2022[12]), a definition also adopted by existing OECD work in this space (OECD, 2021[13]; 2021[14]; 2023[15]). Mental health is more than the absence of a clinically diagnosed mental health condition; mental health can be conceptualised on a single continuum of experience (from severe mental ill-health to positive mental health), or, as is increasingly done, as a dual continuum in which mental ill-health and positive mental states are related, but distinct, experiences (refer to OECD (2023[15]) to for an extended discussion).

Population mental health measures capture the persistence of moods, emotions and affective states over an explicit reference period, often the past two or four weeks. Experiencing negative emotions is not indicative of a mental health condition – this is a normal and healthy part of life – however, the persistence of these emotions over a longer duration of time suggests the risk of a mental health condition. Therefore while the concepts included in these mental health scales overlap with emotional states that also appear in affect modules (Box 2.5), the question formulations are different: the reference period is longer – to capture persistent states – and many tools have been validated against clinical diagnoses of specific mental health conditions (in particular, major depressive disorder and generalised anxiety disorder, the two most commonly occurring mental health conditions). For this reason, the data obtained from these tools should be used and interpreted differently from the data resulting from a measure of affect balance. Refer to Box A A.1 in the Annex for a discussion of the differences between affect and mental health measurement and the policy applications of both.

The population mental health extended module includes a general overall assessment of the respondent's mental health (Q1); a mental health screening tool to assess the risk for depression and anxiety, using the Patient Health Questionnaire-4 (Q2-5); and an assessment of positive mental health, using the WHO-5 Well-being Index (Q6-10) (Box 2.7). These recommendations appear in *Measuring Population Mental Health* (OECD, 2023[15]).

Box 2.7. Population mental health extended module

Q1. In general, how is your mental health? [Excellent; very good; good; fair; poor]

[Patient Health Questionnaire-4 (PHQ-4)]

Over the last two weeks, how often have you been bothered by any of the following problems. When thinking about "how often", please choose from the following options: not at all; several days; more than half the days; nearly every day.

Q2. Feeling nervous, anxious or on edge

Q3. Not being able to stop or control worrying

Q4. Feeling down, depressed or hopeless

Q5. Little interest or pleasure in doing things

[WHO-5 Well-being Index (WHO-5)]

Over the past two weeks, how often have you felt the following. When thinking about "how often", please choose from the following options: all of the time; most of the time; more than half the time; less than half the time; some of the time; at no time.

Q6. I have felt cheerful and in good spirits

Q7. I have felt calm and relaxed

Q8. I have felt active and vigorous

Q9. I woke up feeling fresh and rested

Q10. My daily life has been filled with things that interest me

Implementation details:

- The questions in the module should be fielded using the exact phrasing and answer formats provided. Questions are designed be used as a set and asked in the order in which they appear. Given limited space, only Q2-Q5 (the PHQ-4) can be asked. If implemented in full, it is recommended to include a brief transition statement between the PHQ-4 (Q2-Q4) and the WHO-5 (Q6-Q10).
- The PHQ-4 screening tool (Q2-5) is a short, four-question tool to identify the presence and severity of core symptoms of both depression and anxiety, given that these are two of the most prevalent mental health illnesses among the general population and are often comorbid.
  - The PHQ-4 pulls the two, core depression-related questions from the longer Patient Health Questionnaire (which together are called the PHQ-2), plus two core anxiety-related questions from Generalized Anxiety Disorder (GAD)-7 (which are called the GAD-2).
  - For survey designers with sufficient space, it is recommended to field the full length, eight-item Patient Health Questionnaire (PHQ-8) survey and the full length seven-item Generalized Anxiety Disorder (GAD-7) survey. The full questionnaires and scoring conventions of both are outlined in detail in Annex 2.B of *Measuring Population Mental Health* (OECD, 2023[15]).

- The World Health Organization Well-Being Index (WHO-5) is a short questionnaire of five items that focus on a respondent's positive affect. The questionnaire was first used in a project on well-being measures in primary health care by the WHO Regional Office in Europe in 1998 and since then has been translated into more than 30 languages. The WHO-5 has been applied as a generic scale for well-being across a wide range of study fields and countries and also as a sensitive screening tool for depression in clinical trials. For more detail, refer to Annex 2.B of *Measuring Population Mental Health* (OECD, 2023[15]).

Time:

- This module is expected to take about 4 minutes to complete in its entirety.

Origin:

- This set of recommendations appears in (OECD, 2023[15]).
- Q1 is fielded by Statistics Canada (Statistics Canada, 2024[16]).
- Q2-4 make up the Patient Health Questionnaire-4 (Kroenke et al., 2009[17]). The full-length Patient Health Questionnaire (PHQ-8) and the WHO-5 are both included in the European Health Interview Survey, fielded in EU countries every five to six years. Detailed implementation instructions can be found in Eurostat (2024[18]). Additionally, the PHQ-8 and GAD-7 are included in on-going OECD Health Division work to monitor mental health system performance (OECD, forthcoming[19]).
- Q6-10 make up the WHO-5 Wellbeing Index (Topp et al., 2015[20]). The WHO-5 Index has been translated into multiple languages; questionnaires in 29 different languages can be downloaded at: https://www.who.int/publications/m/item/WHO-UCN-MSD-MHE-2024.01.

Output:

- Q1 can be reported as the share of the population reporting each answer option ("excellent", "very good", "good", "fair", "poor"), omitting missing values. In addition, rather than report a deprivation, the share of respondents who report having "excellent" or "very good" mental health should be reported jointly as a measure of positive mental health.
- The Patient Health Questionnaire-4 should be scored as follows:
  - Each answer option is assigned the following numerical value: not at all = 0; several days = 1; more than half the days = 2; nearly every day = 3.
  - All items are added together to provide a total score of psychological distress ranging from 0-12, with higher scores indicating the presence of more symptomatology: 0-2 normal, 3-5 mild, 6-8 moderate and 9-12 severe.
  - Missing values should not be imputed. If one of the two questions comprising the depression component of the scale is missing (Q4 or Q5), the risk for depression should not be calculated; however, if both questions comprising the anxiety component of the scale are present (Q2 and Q3), the risk for anxiety can be calculated. The same is true vice versa, should both depression questions be present, but one anxiety item is missing.
  - A total score greater than or equal to 3 for the first two items (GAD-2) indicates that the respondent is at risk for generalised anxiety. A total score greater than or equal to 3 for the final two items (PHQ-2) indicates that the respondent is at risk for depression. Data producers can then report on the share of the population at risk for psychological distress, at risk for anxiety and at risk for depression, respectively.
- The WHO-5 Well-being Index should be scored as follows:
  - Each answer option is assigned the following numerical value: all of the time = 5; most of the time = 4; more than half the time = 3; less than half the time = 2; some of the time = 1; and at no time = 0.

- If any one of the five items is missing, the overall score cannot be calculated, and all values should be treated as missing.
- All items are added together to provide a total score from 0 to 25, which is then multiplied by 4 to normalise to a score of 0 (worst possible well-being) to 100 (best possible well-being). Data producers can report the mean value; the mean value of responses, and the standard error of this estimate, can be used to describe differences between population groups.
- The percentage of the population reporting scores below a threshold (a score < 50) can also be reported to indicate the share of the population experiencing "low levels of positive mental health".
- It is not recommended to present the answers to individual scale items to provide information on a particular emotional state. Data producers interested in doing so should instead refer to measures of affect (Box 2.5).

Guidelines for interviewers:

- Q1 is intended to capture how people evaluate their mental health in general and does not refer to a specific time period.
- Q2-10 refer to the previous two weeks and, as such, are designed to capture the persistence of each emotional state.
- For Q2-Q10, if a respondent reports feeling the emotion only one day over the past two weeks, the output should be coded as "Not at all", rather than "Several days". If the respondent felt the emotion for two days, this should be coded as "Several days". This aligns with protocols outlined by Eurostat (2024[18]).
- Visual aids may be needed to remind respondents of the different answer options for each question set. For phone-based surveys, additional prompting and reminders may be necessary.

Time use surveys

The preceding survey modules in this chapter are designed to be integrated into household surveys. Time use surveys, on the other hand, provide data on how people spend their time, how long they spend on different types of activities and who they spend their time with. Increasingly, time use surveys are used to provide important insights into unpaid labour and care work (UNSD, 2025[21]; Tchipeva, Miceli and Ninka, 2024[22]), and they can also be very valuable in understanding relational components of well-being, such as time spent socialising (OECD, 2024[23]).

Subjective well-being data can, and have been, integrated into time use surveys and are especially well suited for collecting data on affect. Refer to Annex A for a discussion of how affect measures – and in particular those collected in time use diaries – are relevant for policy. Since measures of affect aim to capture information on how a respondent actually feels in a given moment, affect data collected via time use surveys are considered the gold standard in measuring directly experienced emotions and states through population surveys. Because countries have varied approaches to fielding time use surveys – and many are in the process of updating and digitising these surveys – further options, in addition to the one shown in the module below, are provided for interested data producers in Annex A. Practical examples of how national statistical offices have implemented the different approaches are also shown.

Time use diary measurement

Time use diary measurement captures information on how the respondent feels directly in the time use diary alongside information on the activities a respondent engaged in the day prior, whom they were with and where they were. This approach – shown in Box 2.8 – includes one question (Q1) asking respondents to rate how pleasant or unpleasant each specific activity was, which can be integrated into an existing time use diary (see Figure 2.2 for an example).

The primary question on overall satisfaction with life (Q1 in the core module, Box 2.2) should also be asked as part of the time use survey.

Box 2.8. Time use diary measurement

Q1. Was this moment pleasant or unpleasant? (see right column in figure below)
[from -3 (very unpleasant) to +3 (very pleasant)]

Figure 2.2. Full time use diary method

Time	***What were you doing?*** *Record your main activity for each 10-minute period from 07.00 to 10.00. Only one main activity on each line. Distinguish between travel and the activity that is the reason for travelling.*	***What else were you doing?*** *Record the most important parallel activity.*	***Did you use a computer, smartphone, tablet, or similar device for doing this?***	***Where were you?*** *Record the location or the mode of transport. E.g. at home, at a friend's home, at school, at workplace, in restaurant, in shop, on foot, on bicycle, in car, on motorbike, on bus, …*	***Were you alone or together with someone you know?*** ***Mark "yes" by crossing***						***Was this moment pleasant or unpleasant?*** *(from -3 - very unpleasant, to +3 - very pleasant)*
			Yes		Alone (or with unknown persons)	With other household members: Partner	Parent	Children (up to 17 years)	Other household member	Other persons that you know	
07:00-07:10	*Woke up the children*		☐	*At home*	☐	☐	☐	☒	☐	☐	-1
07:10-07:20	*Had breakfast*	*Talked with my family*	☐	↓	☐	☒	☐	☒	☐	☐	3
07:20-07:30	–"–	–"–	☐		☐	☒	☐	☒	☐	☐	3
07:30-07:40	*Cleared the table*	*Listened to the radio*	☒		☐	☒	☐	☐	☐	☐	1
07:40-07:50	*Helped the children dress*	*Talked with my children*	☐		☐	☐	☐	☒	☐	☐	1
07:50-08:00	*Went to the day care centre*	–"–	☐	*On foot*	☐	☐	☐	☒	☐	☐	1
08:00-08:10	*Went to work*	*Read the newspaper*	☒	*Bus*	☒	☐	☐	☒	☐	☐	-1
08:10-08:20	–"–	–"–	☒	–"–	☒	☐	☐	☐	☐	☐	-1
08:20-08:30	*Work*	–"–	☒	*Workplace*	☒	☐	☐	☐	☐	☐	0
08:30-08:40	↓	*Meeting with boss*	☐	↓	☐	☐	☐	☐	☐	☒	0
08:40-08:50		–"–	☐		☐	☐	☐	☐	☐	☒	0
08:50-09:00		–"–	☐		☐	☐	☐	☐	☐	☒	0
09:00-09:10			☒		☒	☐	☐	☐	☐	☐	2
09:10-09:20			☒		☒	☐	☐	☐	☐	☐	2
09:20-09:30			☒		☒	☐	☐	☐	☐	☐	2
09:30-09:40			☒		☒	☐	☐	☐	☐	☐	2
09:40-09:50			☒		☒	☐	☐	☐	☐	☐	2
09:50-10:00			☒		☒	☐	☐	☐	☐	☐	2

Use an arrow, citation marks or the like to mark an activity that takes longer than 10 minutes.

Source: Adapted, to include a subjective well-being question, from Eurostat (2020[24]), *Harmonised European Time Use Surveys: 2018 Guidelines: Re-edition, 2020 edition*, https://ec.europa.eu/eurostat/web/products-manuals-and-guidelines/-/ks-gq-20-011.

Implementation details:

- Q1 should be answered as a part of the time use diary, so that respondents capture information on how pleasant/unpleasant an activity is, as soon after that activity as possible.

Time:

- Q1 is expected to add an extra 5 minutes to the time it takes respondents to complete the time use diary (OECD, 2013[25]).

Origin:

- Q1 was included in the original *Guidelines*, and is the formulation currently used by the Italian national statistical office. Additionally, the Finnish statistical office uses a version of this question, supplemented by a visual aid, and it has been used by the French statistical office in previous time use surveys (refer to the Annex for details).

Output:

- Information derived from Q1 is conceptually similar to calculating an affect balance (see Box 2.5). Responses to Q1 can also be presented as the mean score for different activity types or the mean score for different demographic groups (e.g. sex, age groups, labour force status).
- It is also possible to construct a U-index (unpleasantness index) from this data (Kahneman and Krueger, 2006[26]), calculated as the proportion of time when the net affect associated with an activity is positive (i.e. >= 0).

Guidelines for interviewers:

- These questions relate to how the respondent felt during a specific episode identified from a time use diary. It is important that the respondent answers with respect to how they felt during the period of time covered by that episode rather than providing information on how they felt during the day as a whole or what the dominant emotion was during the day.

References

Clark, A. (2001), "What really matters in a job? Hedonic measurement using quit data", *Labour Economics*, Vol. 8/2, pp. 223-242, https://doi.org/10.1016/S0927-5371(01)00031-8. [4]

Clark, A., Y. Georgellis and P. Sanfey (1999), "Job satisfaction, wage changes and Quits: Evidence from Germany", SSRN, https://papers.ssrn.com/abstract=132109. [5]

Cummins, R. (ed.) (2024), *Personal Wellbeing Index Manual*, Australian Centre on Quality of Life, School of Psychology, Deakin University – Melbourne Campus, https://www.acqol.com.au/uploads/pwi-a/pwi-a-english.pdf. [7]

Eurostat (2024), *European Health Interview Survey wave 4 – Methodological manual – 2024 edition*, European Commission, https://ec.europa.eu/eurostat/web/products-manuals-and-guidelines/w/ks-gq-24-018. [18]

Eurostat (2020), *Harmonised European Time Use Surveys : 2018 Guidelines : Re-edition, 2020 edition*, https://ec.europa.eu/eurostat/web/products-manuals-and-guidelines/-/ks-gq-20-011. [24]

Kahneman, D. and A. Krueger (2006), "Developments in the measurement of subjective well-being", *Journal of Economic Perspectives*, Vol. 20/1, pp. 3–24, https://doi.org/10.1257/089533006776526030. [26]

Kaiser, C. and A. Oswald (2022), "The scientific value of numerical measures of human feelings", *PNAS*, Vol. 119/42, https://doi.org/10.1073/pnas.2210412119. [3]

Kroenke, K. et al. (2009), "An ultra-brief screening scale for anxiety and depression: The PHQ-4", *Psychosomatics*, Vol. 50/6, pp. 613-621, https://doi.org/10.1176/APPI.PSY.50.6.613. [17]

Lambert, L. et al. (2020), "Towards a greater global understanding of wellbeing: A proposal for a more inclusive measure", *International Journal of Wellbeing*, Vol. 10/2, pp. 1-18, https://internationaljournalofwellbeing.org/index.php/ijow/article/view/1037/877. [8]

OECD (2024), *How's Life? 2024: Well-being and Resilience in Times of Crisis*, OECD Publishing, Paris, https://doi.org/10.1787/90ba854a-en. [23]

OECD (2023), *Measuring Population Mental Health*, OECD Publishing, Paris, https://doi.org/10.1787/5171eef8-en. [15]

OECD (2021), *A New Benchmark for Mental Health Systems: Tackling the Social and Economic Costs of Mental Ill-Health*, OECD Health Policy Studies, OECD Publishing, Paris, https://doi.org/10.1787/4ed890f6-en. [14]

OECD (2021), *Fitter Minds, Fitter Jobs: From Awareness to Change in Integrated Mental Health, Skills and Work Policies*, Mental Health and Work, OECD Publishing, Paris, https://doi.org/10.1787/a0815d0f-en. [13]

OECD (2013), *OECD Guidelines on Measuring Subjective Well-being*, OECD Publishing, Paris, https://doi.org/10.1787/9789264191655-en. [25]

OECD (forthcoming), *OECD Mental Health Data Pilot, 2025*, OECD Publishing, Paris. [19]

ONS (2024), *UK Measures of National Well-being Dashboard*, Office for National Statistics (ONS), https://www.ons.gov.uk/peoplepopulationandcommunity/wellbeing/articles/ukmeasuresofnationalwellbeing/dashboard. [2]

Powdthavee, N. (2009), "I can't smile without you: Spousal correlation in life satisfaction", *Journal of Economic Psychology*, Vol. 30/4, pp. 675-689, https://doi.org/10.1016/J.JOEP.2009.06.005. [6]

Raja, S. et al. (2020), "The revised International Association for the Study of Pain definition of pain: concepts, challenges, and compromises", *Pain*, Vol. 161/9, pp. 1976-1982, https://doi.org/10.1097/J.PAIN.0000000000001939. [1]

Rutherford, L. et al. (2024), *European Social Survey Round 12 Cognitive Interviewing*, National Centre for Social Research, https://europeansocialsurvey.org/sites/default/files/2025-04/natcen-ess12-cognitive-interviewing.pdf. [10]

Ryff, C. and C. Keyes (1995), "The structure of psychological well-being revisited.", *Journal of Personality and Social Psychology*, Vol. 69/4, pp. 719-727, https://doi.org/10.1037/0022-3514.69.4.719. [11]

Statistics Canada (2024), *Quality of life indicator: Self-rated mental health*, Statistics Canada, https://www160.statcan.gc.ca/health-sante/mental-health-sante-mentale-eng.htm. [16]

Statistics Finland (2024), *Citizens' Pulse*, Statistics Finland, https://stat.fi/en/surveys/pulssi. [9]

Tchipeva, T., M. Miceli and E. Ninka (2024), *Time Use Surveys in Europe: State of play and a glimpse into the future*, Eurostat, https://unstats.un.org/unsd/demographic-social/meetings/2024/tus-egm-20240130/Session-2B-c-Eurostat-Eniel-Ninka.pdf (accessed on 14 February 2025). [22]

Topp, C. et al. (2015), "The WHO-5 well-being index: A systematic review of the literature", *Psychotherapy and Psychosomatics*, Vol. 84/3, pp. 167-176, https://doi.org/10.1159/000376585. [20]

UNSD (2025), *Guide to Producing Statistics on Time Use*, United Nations Statistics Division, https://unstats.un.org/UNSDWebsite/statcom/session_55/documents/BG-3k-Guide_to_Producing_Statistics_on_Time_Use-55UNSC_background-E.pdf. [21]

WHO (2022), *Mental Health*, World Health Organization, https://www.who.int/news-room/fact-sheets/detail/mental-health-strengthening-our-response. [12]

3. Cross-cutting experimental module and question banks

This chapter introduces a cross-cutting module of experimental subjective well-being measures that have broad-based relevance across cultures but, as of yet, have not been widely included in large-scale official data collections. These include in particular low arousal positive affect and measures of subjective well-being with a strong relational component. The chapter also provides question banks (rather than a module) for additional important concepts for which existing evidence is insufficient to recommend a single measure that best captures the concept in a valid and concise way. These include balance and harmony in one's life, a connection to future generations and an emotional connection to the natural world. While future work is needed to identify single-item measures that best measure each element, on whole, the inclusion of these measures in subjective well-being modules can enhance the global inclusivity of measurement practice.

A key consideration in the process of refining and updating OECD measurement guidelines on subjective well-being was to ensure that the resulting question modules contain measures that capture well-understood concepts that have meaning and resonate for populations both within and among countries, rather than being too strongly anchored in only some regions, cultures or population groups. Broad relevance is a central objective for any international measurement guidelines, where the goal is to provide sets of measures that can be fielded successfully across different countries and contexts. This objective differs from – but can be very effectively complemented and informed by – national efforts to develop tailored surveys addressing the well-being needs of specific communities (see Box A A.3. in the Annex). Thus, one of the selection criteria for all measures recommended in Chapter 2 is global inclusivity, meaning that the outcomes measured need to have evidence of broad-based resonance and successful deployment in a wide variety of countries and contexts. As a part of the process to ensure this, a technical overview of the global evidence base on subjective well-being measurement was conducted that widened the scope beyond the usual set of academic economics and psychology journals to also include evidence from other sources, with an explicit goal of including evidence from non-OECD countries (Smith et al., 2025[1]).

As well as informing the recommendations in Chapter 2, this exercise highlighted some additional subjective well-being elements that are not currently captured by existing measurement guidelines and that could serve to broaden the global relevance of the recommendations. These elements, included here in Chapter 3, are considered as *cross-cutting experimental* measures for three different, but sometimes overlapping, reasons: (1) evidence on the statistical properties of existing measures to capture these specific elements is minimal, especially extensions to populations (and linguistic groups) outside of the national context in which they were developed; (2) the new elements do not fit neatly into the life evaluation / affect / eudaimonia framework of subjective well-being (Figure 1.2) and may therefore be better thought of as cross-cutting measures, and (3) because there are few examples of single-item measures, or insufficient evidence to propose a specific measure – even if it is deemed experimental – to capture the concept. A cross-cutting module of subjective well-being measures is provided to capture measures falling into the first two categories, while question banks with multiple measurement approaches are provided for the latter.

For official data producers who have a well-established subjective well-being measurement practice, the experimental measures and question banks in this chapter are intended to be a useful resource to expand coverage of important subjective well-being elements that have heretofore remained under-measured and thus under-studied and under-prioritised.

A cross-cutting experimental module of subjective well-being measures

When reviewing the global evidence base on varied approaches to subjective well-being measurement, frequently recurring themes include: a greater diversity of low arousal positive affect measures (beyond feeling calm, which is included in the affect extended module Box 2.5), such as being at peace and feeling content, or a sense of spirituality; and measures of subjective well-being with a strong relational component, that are distinct from typical measures of social connections (Box A A.2) in that they are emotional experiences that can be interpreted only in the context of other people, or they are subjective evaluations of the well-being of a concept broader than the self (e.g. extending to a person's family or the people around them).

These concepts are included in an experimental module of subjective well-being measures (Box 3.1). A detailed discussion on each topic, including more information on the policy relevance of the concept and existing approaches to its measurement, can be found in the Annex. The experimental module is cross-cutting, in that it includes subjective well-being measures that span evaluative, eudaimonic and affective components. The module begins by asking respondents to reflect on how well their family is doing overall (Q1). The next two questions refer to general feelings, asking respondents how often they feel their mind is at ease, a measure of low arousal positive affect (Q2), how often they feel a sense of something bigger than themselves, a question about spirituality that is not specific to any one religious group (Q3), and how often they feel that their actions positively impact others – a measure of beneficence (Q4). The final set of questions asks respondents to report how often they felt the given emotion over the preceding day: treated with respect (Q5), envious (Q6), compassionate (Q7), forgiving (Q8), fearful (Q9), generous (Q10) and selfish (Q11).

Box 3.1. Cross-cutting module of experimental subjective well-being measures

First of all, I'd like you to think in general about how your family is doing.

Q1. On a scale of 0 to 10, where zero means "extremely badly" and ten means "extremely well", how would you rate how your family is doing these days? [0-10; I have no family]

The following questions ask about your feelings in general. Zero means you did not experience the feeling "at all", while 10 means you experience the feeling "all of the time". On a scale from 0 to 10, in general how often:

Q2. ... is your mind at ease? [0-10]

Q3. ... do you feel a sense of connection to something bigger than yourself? [0-10]

Q4. ... do you feel that your actions have a positive impact on the people around you? [0-10]

The following questions ask about how you felt yesterday on a scale from 0 to 10. Zero means you did not experience the feeling "at all" yesterday while 10 means you experienced the feeling "all of the time" yesterday. Here is a list of ways you might have felt yesterday.

Q5. How about that you were treated with respect? [0-10]

Q6. How about envious? [0-10]

Q7. How about compassionate? [0-10]

Q8. How about forgiving? [0-10]

Q9. How about fearful? [0-10]

Q10. How about generous? [0-10]

Q11. How about selfish? [0-10]

Implementation details:

- The questions in the module should be fielded using the exact phrasing and answer formats provided. Questions selected by data producers should be asked in the order in which they appear. Given limited space, survey designers can ask only Q1-Q7. The module can be implemented alongside the core module (Box 2.2).
- All questions are deemed experimental; more information on why these measures have been selected, and the importance of each concept, can be found in Annex A.
- Q5-11 use a yesterday recall period, which enables them to be used alongside measures in the affect extended module (Box 2.5). Should space be a constraint, Q5, Q6 and Q7 should be prioritised for inclusion alongside the affect extended module.

Time:

- This module is expected to take between 4 and 5 minutes to complete in its entirety.

Origin:

- Q1 is originally from the New Zealand General Social Survey (Statistics New Zealand, 2024[2]), which was itself adapted from a question that was originally developed for Te Kupenga, a survey of social, cultural and economic well-being of the Indigenous Māori population in New Zealand (Statistics New Zealand, 2014[3]).
- Q2 is from the Gallup World Poll Wellbeing module (Lomas et al., 2022[4]); the answer scale has been adapted to a 0-10 format.
- Q3 is a single item of the longer Spiritual Well-Being: The Awe Index scale (Hamby, Grych and Banyard, 2013[5]); the answer scale has been adapted to a 0-10 scale to align with other measures in the module.
- Q4 is a single item in the Beneficence Scale (Martela and Ryan, 2016[6]) and has been adapted to use a 0-10 answer scale.
- Q5 has been adapted from a Gallup question fielded in its annual World Poll (Gallup World Poll, 2024[7]).
- Q6-11 are originally from the Bhutan Gross National Happiness Survey (Ura et al., 2022[8]); they have been adapted to use a 0-10 answer scale and yesterday recall period.

Output:

- Information on individual questions can be presented as the mean value of each response, omitting missing values. Summary measures of distribution (inequalities) should also be reported (see Box 1.2 for details). The mean value of responses, and the standard error of this estimate, can be used to describe differences between population groups.
- The percentage of the population reporting scores below a "low outcome" threshold (a score ≤ 4) can also be reported.

Guidelines for interviewers:

- Q1-4 deliberately focus on how people are feeling in general rather than specifying a longer or shorter time period, and they ask the respondents for a reflective judgement rather than a statement of their current mood.
- For Q1, respondents should consider all areas of life when rating how well their family is doing. Family refers to the group of people that respondents think of as their family. Some official data producers may have pre-established definitions as to what constitutes "family", in those instances those same criteria can be applied here, with respondents prompted as necessary.
- Q3 is a question about spirituality, but to ensure broad relevance, it does not mention a god or formal religion and rather focuses on the existential dimension of spirituality.
- As for Q5-11, the aim of the module is to capture information on respondents' feelings, states, moods or emotions on the previous day. The time frame is explicitly short because the primary focus is the affective states that people actually experienced, which is most accurately recalled over short time periods. If a respondent indicates that the previous day was unusual in some respect (something particularly bad or good happened, or they were feeling unwell), they should still report how they felt that day, since this question is intended to capture the feelings people have actually experienced, not how people feel on a "typical" day. These affect items are designed to be used in very large sample household surveys only under these conditions; because several thousand people are be interviewed over a relatively long period of time over the course of the survey, unusual events will not overly bias the aggregated statistics that are produced. More

importantly, the reference to a specific day permits the data to be used to unravel day-of-week effects and responses to external events for which the dates are known.

Question banks for additional subjective well-being concepts

The scoping exercise on globally inclusive approaches to subjective well-being measurement yielded additional important concepts for which different measurement approaches exist. However, these measures vary in question framing and length. These concepts include a feeling of balance and/or harmony in one's life, feeling connected to future generations (in a broad sense, beyond feeling concern or consideration for one's own children or grandchildren, personally) and feeling connected to nature. Given the lack of existing evidence on the statistical properties of these, there is thus far insufficient information to provide a single recommended measure. Instead, question banks showing some of the most prominent existing measures are provided so that interested data producers can select, and adapt, the options that are best suited to their national (or local) context. Given the current lack of evidence, fielding and testing these questions – and publishing the results – will be a crucial tool in improving the evidence base.

Balance and harmony

Balance and harmony are highly interrelated concepts that touch on feeling that the various forces in one's life are in equilibrium. These concepts have so far largely been absent from subjective well-being measurement conversations despite their universal relevance and strong link to concepts of happiness and satisfaction (refer to Annex A for an extended discussion). Table 3.1 provides examples of measures capturing balance and harmony. Beginning in 2020, the Gallup World Poll has included measures of both balance and harmony in its well-being module. Cognitive testing has yielded some insights into which measures are better understood than others (refer to Annex A for details); however, there is not yet consensus as to which measure is best placed to capture harmony and balance. In addition to Gallup's work, the Harmony in Life Scale – both the full-length and shorter versions – provides a multi-item scale approach to measurement.

Table 3.1. Balance and harmony question bank

Question	Answer scale	Source
In general, how often: ... are the various aspects of your life in balance? ... do you feel that the amount of things happening in your life is just right – not too much or too little? ... are you in harmony with those around you? ... are your thoughts and feelings in harmony? ... are your actions in harmony with your personal values?	Always, often, rarely, never	(Lomas et al., 2022[4])
Harmony in Life Scale My lifestyle allows me to be in harmony Most aspects of my life are in balance I am in harmony I accept the various conditions of my life I fit in well with my surroundings	1 (strongly disagree) to 7 (strongly agree)	(Kjell et al., 2016[9])
Harmony in Life Scale (short) My lifestyle allows me to be in harmony Most aspects of my life are in balance I am in harmony	1 (strongly disagree) to 7 (strongly agree)	(Kjell and Diener, 2021[10])

Connection to future generations

A sense of connection to one's ancestors and descendants is a common feature in many Indigenous well-being frameworks, and, increasingly, OECD member state governments are introducing policies and legislative frameworks focused on the well-being of future generations (see Annex A). Different ways to measure affinity towards future generations are shown in Table 3.2. The first three rows show different ways to frame single-item questions: being in harmony with the needs of future generations, an evaluative assessment of what life will be like for future generations, and satisfaction with the younger generation's future. One multi-item scale is also included.

Table 3.2. Connection to future generations question bank

Question	Answer scale	Source
The following question asks about your feelings in general. Zero means you did not experience the feeling "at all", while 10 means you experience the feeling "all of the time". On a scale from 0 to 10, in general how often: ... are you in harmony with the needs of future generations?	0-10	(Smith et al., 2025[1])
How do you think life in France will be for the next generation? How do you think life will be in other European countries for the next generation?	0-10	(CEPREMAP, 2025[11])
How satisfied are you today with the following areas of your life? Please rate them from 0 (completely dissatisfied) to 10 (completely satisfied). [Young generation's future]	0-10	(LiK, 2025[12])
Social Generativity Scale: I carry out activities in order to ensure a better world for future generations I have a personal responsibility to improve the area in which I live I give up part of my daily comforts to foster the development of future generations I think that I am responsible for ensuring a state of well-being for future generations I commit myself to do things that will survive even after I die I help people to improve themselves	1 (strongly disagree) to 7 (strongly agree)	(Morselli and Passini, 2015[13])

Connection with nature

Connection with nature is distinct from measures that describe the quality or features of the natural environment, or the amount of time one spends in nature. Rather, this concept recognises that in some traditions there is not a clear distinction between the self and nature and that many cultures place value on being connected to, and in harmony with, the natural world (Annex A). Unlike the preceding two concepts, the evidence base on existing measures is more extensive for connection to nature – but these measures have been developed to address people's value systems, not their subjective well-being. In addition, validated single-item measures (or ultra-brief scales) are lacking. The Gallup World Poll provides possible examples of single-item measures, asking respondents how emotionally connected they feel to nature (fielded in 2021) and how often they feel in harmony with nature around them (fielded in 2024) (Table 3.3). Experimentation with phrasing to ensure face validity is on-going at the time of this publication. In addition, the Inclusion of Nature in Self Scale is a single-item question that uses a visual aid to enable respondents to assess their perceived closeness to nature (Figure 3.1); it is a single-item scale, however, the visual component makes it inappropriate for telephone-based surveys.

Beyond this, the 14-item Connectedness to Nature Scale is one of the most referenced in the literature; however, its length makes it difficult to integrate into general household surveys (Mayer and Frantz, 2004[14]). Three other multi-item scales – the Environmental Identity Scale, the Love and Care for Nature Scale (Perkins, 2010[15]) and the Nature Relatedness Scale (Mayer and Frantz, 2004[14]) – also frequently appear. The *Practitioner Guide to Assessing Connection to Nature* includes details on how to implement such scales, as well as how to analyse and report on the data once collected (Salazar, Kunkle and Monroe, 2020[16]).

Table 3.3. Connection with nature question bank

Question	Answer scale	Source
In general, how often do you feel each of the following? --- emotionally connected to nature For this next question, please think about the natural environment, such as plants, animals and water. In general, how often do you feel you are in harmony with nature around you?	Always, often, rarely, never	(Lomas et al., 2022[4])

Figure 3.1. Inclusion of Nature in Self Scale

Please circle the picture that best describes your relationship with the natural environment. How interconnected are you with nature?

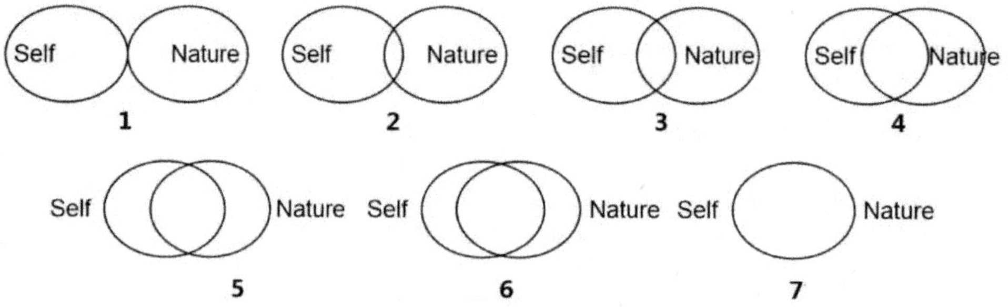

Note: A respondent's score is the numerical value associated with the image selected; the overall score can then be calculated as the mean value of all response outcomes.

Source: Schultz (2002[17]), "Inclusion with Nature: The Psychology Of Human-Nature Relations", *Psychology of Sustainable Development*, pp. 61-78, https://doi.org/10.1007/978-1-4615-0995-0_4; image taken from Chen et al. (2022[18]), "The Impact of Gratitude on Connection With Nature: The Mediating Role of Positive Emotions of Self-Transcendence", *Frontiers in Psychology*, Vol. 13, p. 908138, https://doi.org/10.3389/FPSYG.2022.908138.

References

CEPREMAP (2025), *Le Bien-Être en France*, https://www.cepremap.fr/Tableau_de_Bord_Bien-Etre.html. [11]

Chen, L. et al. (2022), "The impact of gratitude on connection with nature: The mediating role of positive emotions of self-transcendence", *Frontiers in Psychology*, Vol. 13, p. 908138, https://doi.org/10.3389/FPSYG.2022.908138. [18]

Gallup World Poll (2024), *The State of Global Emotions*, https://www.gallup.com/analytics/349280/gallup-global-emotions-report.aspx. [7]

Hamby, S., J. Grych and V. Banyard (2013), *Life paths measurement packet: finalized Scales*, https://lifepathsresearch.org/wp-content/uploads/2021/10/Life-Paths-Measurement-Packet-finalized-scales-Aug-2015-Color-front-and-back.pdf. [5]

Kjell, O. et al. (2016), "The Harmony in Life Scale complements the Satisfaction with Life Scale: Expanding the conceptualization of the cognitive component of subjective well-being", *Social Indicators Research*, Vol. 126/2, pp. 893-919, https://doi.org/10.1007/S11205-015-0903-Z. [9]

Kjell, O. and E. Diener (2021), "Abbreviated three-item versions of the Satisfaction with Life Scale and the Harmony in Life Scale yield as strong psychometric properties as the original scales", *Journal of Personality Assessment*, Vol. 103/2, pp. 183-194, https://doi.org/10.1080/00223891.2020.1737093. [10]

LiK (2025), *The 'Life in Kyrgyzstan' Study*, Life in Kyrgyzstan (LiK), https://lifeinkyrgyzstan.org/. [12]

Lomas, T. et al. (2022), "Balance and harmony in the Gallup World Poll: The development of the Global Wellbeing Initiative module", *International Journal of Wellbeing*, Vol. 12/4, pp. 1-19, https://doi.org/10.5502/IJW.V12I4.2655. [4]

Martela, F. and R. Ryan (2016), "The benefits of benevolence: Basic psychological needs, beneficence, and the enhancement of well-being", *Journal of Personality*, Vol. 84/6, pp. 750-764, https://doi.org/10.1111/JOPY.12215. [6]

Mayer, F. and C. Frantz (2004), "The connectedness to nature scale: A measure of individuals' feeling in community with nature", *Journal of Environmental Psychology*, Vol. 24/4, pp. 503-515, https://doi.org/10.1016/J.JENVP.2004.10.001. [14]

Morselli, D. and S. Passini (2015), "Measuring prosocial attitudes for future generations: The social generativity scale", *Journal of Adult Development*, Vol. 22/3, pp. 173-182, https://doi.org/10.1007/S10804-015-9210-9. [13]

Perkins, H. (2010), "Measuring love and care for nature", *Journal of Environmental Psychology*, Vol. 30/4, pp. 455-463, https://doi.org/10.1016/J.JENVP.2010.05.004. [15]

Salazar, G., K. Kunkle and M. Monroe (2020), *Practitioner Guide to Assessing Connection to Nature*, North American Association for Environmental Education, Washington, DC, https://naaee.org/sites/default/files/2022-10/Assessing%20Connection%20to%20Nature.5.6.20.pdf. [16]

Schultz, P. (2002), "Inclusion with nature: The psychology of human-nature relations", *Psychology of Sustainable Development*, pp. 61-78, https://doi.org/10.1007/978-1-4615-0995-0_4. [17]

Smith, C. et al. (2025), “Globally inclusive measures of subjective wellbeing: Updated evidence to inform national data collections”, *OECD Papers on Well-being and Inequalities*, Vol. 35, https://doi.org/10.1787/bd72752a-en (accessed on 11 February 2025). [1]

Statistics New Zealand (2024), *Wellbeing Statistics: 2023*, Statistics New Zealand, https://www.stats.govt.nz/information-releases/wellbeing-statistics-2023/. [2]

Statistics New Zealand (2014), *Te Kupenga 2013 (English)*, Statistics New Zealand, https://www.stats.govt.nz/information-releases/te-kupenga-2013-english. [3]

Ura, K. et al. (2022), *GNH 2022*, Centre for Bhutan & GNH Studies, Thimphu, Bhutan, https://ophi.org.uk/sites/default/files/2024-03/Bhutan_GNH_2022_%282023%29_compressed.pdf. [8]

Annex A. Updating and streamlining OECD recommendations on subjective well-being measurement: Process and evidence

The Annex provides more details on the process of finalising the second edition of the *OECD Guidelines on Measuring Subjective Well-being*, first, by defining the scope of the update and describing the series of working papers that support the recommendations in this report. The rest of the Annex provides details on each of the modules presented in Chapters 2 and 3, giving additional background context on the importance of each conceptual area to be measured and details on the statistical properties for the measures selected to capture each concept. It then explains the decisions that went into determining the measure composition of each module.

Motivation and process of updating the 2013 OECD *Guidelines*

When the *OECD Guidelines on Measuring Subjective Well-being* were first published in 2013, few OECD countries were measuring aspects of subjective well-being in official statistics. While there had been growing recognition of the concept's importance to societal well-being, in particular following the Stiglitz-Sen-Fitoussi report, which specifically noted that "it is possible to collect meaningful and reliable data on subjective well-being" (Stiglitz, Sen and Fitoussi, 2009[1]), in practice this was not done with a great deal of frequency, and even less so in a standardised way – in part because it was not clear how data producers should go about operationalising this advice. The *OECD Guidelines*, then, sought to bring all of the existing evidence together in one place, to clarify the conceptual framing and definition of subjective well-being, to evaluate what is known about the validity and reliability of existing measures, to analyse the effects of different question phrasing and answer scales on response patterns, to understand methodological considerations specific to subjective well-being measures, to clarify how subjective well-being data can (and should) be analysed and used once collected, and, finally, to introduce a core module of standardised measures. Extended modules were also presented, to provide interested data producers with additional measurement options.

The resulting publication not only provided national statistical offices with a wealth of knowledge on the rigour and robustness of subjective well-being data, but by providing a core module with five measures, it also gave interested data producers a set of clear and practical steps to integrate subjective well-being into existing measurement practice. The 2013 edition of the *Guidelines* was intended to be the first step in advancing the subjective well-being measurement agenda, and indeed, as it stated (OECD, 2013, p. 20[2]):

> *These guidelines do not aim to provide the "final word' on the measurement of subjective well-being ... It is envisaged that these guidelines will be followed up by a review of progress on the measurement of subjective well-being over the next few years, with a view to deciding whether the guidelines need revising and whether it is possible and desirable to move towards a greater degree of international standardisation. The intent is that this review will build on information collected by national statistical agencies.*

The review process that resulted in these updated guidelines began in 2023 and, in keeping with the intent of the 2013 *Guidelines*, sought to understand how useful the 2013 recommendations had been to national statistical offices: had more OECD Member countries begun collecting subjective well-being data in official surveys, with greater frequency? Had the recommended measures in the core module been taken up by official data producers? And if the answers to the previous two questions were negative, how could the OECD better refine and clarify its recommendations to make them more useful?

The results of this scoping exercise are outlined in detail in "Subjective well-being measurement: Current practice and new frontiers" (Mahoney, 2023[3]) and can be summarised by four main findings:

- As of 2023, a large share of OECD countries not only measure subjective well-being, but consider it an important component of overall well-being, as evidenced by the inclusion of subjective well-being measure(s) in 20 of the 27 (74%) national well-being initiatives developed by Member states.
- The definition of subjective well-being and the conceptual framework proposed by the guidelines – identifying three components of subjective well-being, covering life evaluation, affect and eudaimonia – have also been widely adopted (Exton, Mahoney and Smith, 2024[4]).
- Measurement of life satisfaction – the primary measure recommended in the original guidelines – has been largely harmonised, with 89% of OECD countries collecting that data in official statistics.
- Measurement practices for affect and eudaimonia are more mixed. Almost all countries measure the affective states that had been recommended in the original guidelines; however, they used a variety of different tools and measurement approaches (including tools designed to assess mental health). Fewer countries measure the eudaimonic concept recommended in the original guidelines (feeling that the things one does in life are worthwhile); however, of those that *did* measure the concept, most all did so using the OECD recommended question.

The review process also took stock of advances in the academic and grey literature to understand how the subjective well-being evidence base has evolved, given the large number of methodological and empirical publications written in the decade since the original guidelines were published. The review touched on many topics but found that much of the evidence corroborated both the methodological guidance set by the OECD (see Chapter 1 of this report) and the rigour of the core module measures. Readers interested in the below topics can refer to (Mahoney, 2023[3]) for a longer discussion, as these additional topics are not addressed further in this publication:

- *New data sources*, including biometric, social media and (linking subjective well-being outcomes to) administrative data.
- *Methodological issues*, covering validity, response scales, question placement, composite indices and mode effects. The working paper discusses a prominent recent critique of the validity of subjective survey data (Bond and Lang, 2019[5]), describing the specifics of the critique as well as a series of rebuttals from academics in the field (Liu and Netzer, 2023[6]) to demonstrate both the external validity of these measures (Kaiser and Vendrik, 2020[7]; Kaiser and Oswald, 2022[8]; Lindqvist, Östling and Cesarini, 2020[9]) and analytical approaches to address scale use heterogeneity without dismissing the data outright (Benjamin et al., 2023[10]). The consensus from the past decade plus of research is that subjective well-being data are meaningful for policy-relevant outcomes.

"Subjective well-being measurement: Current practice and new frontiers" did, however, identify four thematic areas that a future revision of the guidelines should focus on. Three of these research priorities – clarifying measurement recommendations first, for affect and second, for eudaimonia, and exploring globally inclusive measurement approaches – set the parameters for what was in scope, and out of scope, in the process of drafting and shaping the *OECD Guidelines on Measuring Subjective Well-being (2025 Update)*. The fourth and final thematic area identified – to develop subjective well-being measurement guidelines specific to children and young people – will be covered in a forthcoming, second publication. To address the first three topics in detail, the Secretariat worked with expert consultants to draft detailed working papers (Table A A.1). The recommendations in the resulting papers reflect the views and opinions of the external consultants, but the evidence included in each is referenced throughout this publication and helped to shape the final recommendations.

As with the original edition, the full process of updating the guidelines was a consultative one that involved the contributions of many stakeholders. The project commenced with a public conference on subjective well-being measurement, gathering a broad group of stakeholders to discuss advances in measurement since the publication of the 2013 *Guidelines* and to outline priorities for future measurement work. The OECD Secretariat also convened an informal advisory group of more than twenty experts in the field of subjective well-being, who in aggregate provide a diversity of viewpoints across policy, statistics, academia (including academic disciplines, such as economics, psychology and sociology, among others) and geographic regions. The advisory group met in person on two occasions, once in 2024 and once in 2025 – first to clarify the research agenda and questions to be addressed in the associated working papers, and subsequently to react to an early draft of the updated guidelines publication itself. The work has been conducted under the oversight of the OECD Committee on Statistics and Statistical Policy.

Table A A.1. Topics in scope for the guidelines revision process and associated working papers

Thematic area	Research questions	Associated working paper
Refine measurement of affect	• Which affective states are most policy relevant and therefore most suitable for inclusion in OECD recommendations? • What is the most effective way of framing affect questions in terms of recall period? What is the most suitable survey vehicle for affect items? • To what extent do mental health screening tools overlap with affect measures in practice, and how can OECD recommendations better delineate between the two concepts to provide clear guidance?	(Kudrna et al., 2024[11])
Seek a clearer definition of, and meaningful set of measures for, eudaimonia	• How has eudaimonia been defined in the literature, and what are the most important constructs to include in (a) measure(s) of eudaimonia? • How have these constructs been operationalised in household surveys or official statistics? • Is the original guidelines-recommended measure a robust and policy-relevant suggestion, or might there be other eudaimonic constructs that should supplement this measure?	(Abdallah and Mahoney, 2024[12])
Explore more globally inclusive approaches to measurement	• To what extent is the existing subjective well-being literature and evidence base broadly inclusive, or do the findings pull from (globally) non-inclusive populations? • By broadening the scope of evidence to include a greater diversity of regions, ethnic and cultural minority groups, and Indigenous populations, what additional measurement approaches are unearthed, and are there any recurring concepts that do not yet appear in OECD recommendations? • What is known about good practice for data producers when measuring subjective well-being in Indigenous or minority populations?	(Smith et al., 2025[13])

Changes made to the core module

The core module of subjective well-being measures (Box 2.2) differs from the one in the 2013 *Guidelines* in two ways: it includes a new measure on pain, and it removes three questions on affect. The primary subjective well-being measure, which asks respondents how satisfied with their life they feel on average (Q1), remains the same, as does a eudaimonic question on measuring the extent to which respondents feel that the things they do in their life are worthwhile (Q2). Shortening the core module by two questions reduces both respondent burden and implementation cost, and in doing so can increase the likelihood of its wider adoption and higher frequency of its implementation.

Addition of pain

The key change made to the core module is the removal of three affect questions with a "yesterday" recall period, asking respondents how much they experienced being happy, worried or depressed on the day prior. It is important to note that these affect questions remain recommended by the OECD as being valid and reliable and yielding policy-relevant insights, and interested survey designers can find them in the affect extended module (Box 2.5). Similarly, national statistical agencies who currently field affect yesterday questions as a part of their subjective well-being module can and should continue to do so.

These questions were removed from the core module for two primary reasons. First, because yesterday recall periods require sufficiently large samples sizes to ensure that the aggregate of experiences the day prior yield a representative portrait of affect, regardless of how (a)typical the day had been for each individual respondent. Without sufficiently large samples, the data do not yield valid and reliable estimates. Not all data producers have the resources required to field these large-scale surveys on a regular basis, limiting the applicability of "yesterday" recall period questions to a smaller range of surveys. The core module is designed to be integrated into the widest range of household surveys possible, therefore the measures included in it should be adaptable to a wide range of survey types. Additionally, findings from the OECD scoping work into measurement practice revealed that data producers prefer mental health measures with longer recall periods (Mahoney, 2023[3]). In removing "yesterday" recall items from the core module, the hope is that a larger number of national statistical offices in OECD countries will adopt the full set of measures in the core and capture subjective well-being outcomes more frequently, and that those who are interested will be able to supplement with additional measures from the extended (and experimental) modules.

Second, the core module is designed to be as concise as possible, to enable its wide integration into the largest number of surveys possible and to field subjective well-being questions on at least an annual basis. Efforts were made in this edition of the *Guidelines* to streamline recommendations wherever possible. The selected measures for life evaluation (Q1 in Box 2.2) and eudaimonia (Q2 in Box 2.2) represent a single question that best summarises that specific component of subjective well-being. Affect, on the other hand, is a multidimensional construct made up of various positive and negative states: no single measure can encompass "affect" in its entirety. This resulted in three affect questions in the first edition of the *Guidelines*, to cover both positive and negative states. The approach taken this time is different: rather than include a summary set of measures for affect, a single, well-performing example of affect has been selected. That is, the inclusion of pain is *not* meant to suggest that pain is a stand-in for the overarching construct of affect. Rather, pain is an *example* of an affective state – one that works particularly well as a stand-alone measure based on its performance across the four guiding criteria (Box 2.1): statistical properties, brevity, unique policy relevance and consistency.

Affect encompasses feelings, emotions and states – a broad range of outcomes that includes sensations such as pain. The International Association for the Study of Pain (IASP) defines pain as "An unpleasant sensory and emotional experience associated with, or resembling that associated with, actual or potential tissue damage" (Raja et al., 2020[14]). This makes clear that the *emotional* experience of pain is a key component of the overall sensation. Some evidence has found that feelings of pain stemming from social exclusion, rejection or loss rely on the same neural regions that process physical pain (Eisenberger, 2015[15]). For example, evidence from pharmacology highlights the role opioids play in social bonding, beyond pain relief (Panksepp et al., 1978[16]), and neuroimaging studies of pain have found that feelings of social exclusion or social distress activate physical pain-related regions in the brain (Eisenberger, Lieberman and Williams, 2003[17]; Takahashi et al., 2009[18]). The extent of the overlap between social and physical pain is not fully settled and continues to be debated; however, there is greater agreement that both physical and social pain share "a common experiential element … and that is the affective component of pain" (Eisenberger, 2015, p. 621[15]).

Indeed, literature on (subjective) well-being has historically highlighted the relevance and importance of measuring pain, with increasing prominence in recent years. In its call for the collection of subjective well-being data, the Stiglitz-Sen-Fitoussi Commission specifically noted: "Subjective well-being encompasses three different aspects: cognitive evaluations of one's life, positive emotions (joy, pride), and negative ones (***pain***, anger, worry)" [bold/italics added] (Stiglitz, Sen and Fitoussi, 2009, p. 16[1]). An authoritative report on subjective well-being measurement, with a particular focus on experienced well-being (momentary measures of affect), includes pain within the states and sensations considered: experienced well-being "... is often further divided into positive experiences, which may be characterized by terms such as joy, contentment, and happiness, and negative experiences, which may be characterized by sadness, stress, worry, ***pain***, or suffering" [bold/italics added] (p. 3[19]), and the report concludes with an explicit recommendation that pain be measured ("pain questions should be included in ExWB [experienced well-being] questionnaires, particularly in domains such as health or housing where this information is particularly germane to research and policy questions" (National Research Council, 2013, p. 44[19]). Pain was indeed already included in the first edition of the *Guidelines*, although not as a primary recommended measure. More recently, research stemming from the Harvard-based Global Flourishing Study has explicitly called for the inclusion of pain as a component of subjective well-being measurement (Macchia et al., 2025[20]).

Pain is associated with a range of other policy-relevant outcomes (Kudrna et al., 2024[11]). A high prevalence of pain in the population can lead to a greater strain on health care systems, as pain is associated with worse physical and mental health outcomes, alcoholism, over-prescription of opioids, suicide and premature mortality (Case, Deaton and Stone, 2020[21]; Glei, Stokes and Weinstein, 2020[22]). Pain is also associated with worse labour market outcomes, including declining productivity (Wenig et al., 2009[23]; Gaskin and Richard, 2012[24]). Concerningly, some research has hypothesised that economic worry can lead to (physical) pain (Wiech and Tracey, 2009[25]; Chou, Parmar and Galinsky, 2016[26]), and empirical applications have found evidence to support this theory (Macchia and Oswald, 2021[27]). Given the wide-reaching impacts of pain, there have been calls for governments to monitor it when making assessments about overall societal well-being (Macchia, 2023[28]).

Pain has been assessed in clinical settings for many years using many different instruments whose psychometric properties have been extensively studied (Jensen et al., 1999[29]; Hawker et al., 2011[30]; Jensen and Karoly, 2011[31]). The item included in the core module of these guidelines (Q3) is an adapted form of the Numeric Rating Scale (NRS), for which many iterations exist, including both multi-item scales as well as single-item measures (Correll, 2011[32]). The NRS has been shown to be statistically reliable and valid (Jensen et al., 1999[29]; Jensen and Karoly, 2011[31]), including across various cultural and linguistic groups (Karcioglu et al., 2018[33]).

All iterations of the NRS, including single-item measures, have two key features: the question asks about "pain" rather than adding a qualifier (such as "physical", "bodily" or "psychological"), and all use a 0-10 answer scale, where zero represents no pain and ten is the worst pain imaginable. The first point is important, in that this measure does not delineate between "physical" and "mental" pain, since – as the above quoted IASP definition of pain suggests – the experience of pain is both sensory and emotional, and the two are not easily distinguished (Lumley et al., 2011[34]; Gilam et al., 2020[35]; Eisenberger, 2015[15]). In terms of the answer scale, the 0-10 response format aligns with existing OECD recommendations and with other measures in the core module. Additionally, the numeric scale allows data producers to use thresholds in order to group respondents into the categories of "mild", "moderate" and "severe" pain, which can be useful for official data producers when monitoring outcomes over time and comparing across population groups. A lot of literature is devoted to identifying appropriate cut points in the NRS scale, with some small disagreements depending on the desired sensitivity or specificity of the thresholds (Hirschfeld and Zernikow, 2013[36]; Oldenmenger et al., 2013[37]; Alschuler, Jensen and Ehde, 2012[38]). The OECD recommended cut points ("no pain" for a score of 0, "mild" is a score ≥ 1 and ≤ 4; "moderate" (5-6); and "severe" ≥ 7) align with findings from a seminal paper in the pain literature from Serlin et al., (1995[39]), based on a sample of cancer patients. Subsequent studies have extended the cut points to other patient populations, with disagreements over the exact placement of the mild and severe cut-offs. When used in a clinical environment to determine an effective treatment plan, clinicians may want to adapt thresholds to the specific patient population. When monitoring societal pain in the aggregate, on the other hand, it is most important that national statistical offices use a consistent approach to cut-offs – such as the one recommended in the core module reporting instructions.

The single-item NRS pain question used in the core module is a measure that appears on the PROMIS (patient-reported outcomes measurement information system) Adult Short Form survey (HealthMeasures, 2021[40]; Cella et al., 2019[41]). There are many studies assessing the validity and cross-cultural comparability of PROMIS survey measures, including pain, albeit most in clinical settings (Sharma et al., 2021[42]; Rawang et al., 2020[43]; Mahmoud, Rady and Mostafa, 2019[44]). This question is also used in the OECD Patient Reported Indicator Survey (PaRIS), which assesses patients' self-reported views of their experiences with the medical system. The PaRIS survey, and the corresponding pain question, have been successfully fielded in twenty OECD Member states (van den Berg et al., 2024[45]). As official data producers adopt this recommendation and begin fielding the NRS question in non-clinical settings, it is recommended to publish findings on cognitive field testing of the item to show the extent to which respondents understand the question (and its associated prompt) to refer to both physical and mental aspects of pain.

Pain, measured as an affect question – that is, with a short recall period and not phrased as asking about the ways in which pain limits daily activities, an approach used more frequently in health surveys – has been fielded in the annual Gallup World Poll for years (Gallup, n.d.[46]), which has supported academic analysis of the dynamics of pain over time and its broader implications for well-being (Deaton, 2012[47]; Case, Deaton and Stone, 2020[21]; Macchia and Oswald, 2021[27]; Blanchflower and Oswald, 2019[48]). Pain has also been measured in the American Time Use Survey's well-being module, most recently fielded in 2021 (U.S. Bureau of Labor Statistics, 2022[49]), as a part of the UK Office of National Statistics extended experimental experienced well-being questions (ONS, 2011[50]), and is included in the Mexican national statistical office 2025 ENBIARE well-being survey, as a part of the battery of affect items.

The pain measure recommended in the core module here uses a past week recall period (as opposed to yesterday). In general, measures of affect are designed to capture how a respondent is feeling in the moment – or close to it – meaning recall periods should be as short as possible, in part to distinguish these measures from mental health tools (Box A A.1). A past week recall period is used here to enable wider use of this measure, as a part of the core module, including in surveys that do not have sufficiently large sample sizes to ensure valid and reliable measurement of affect yesterday. Unlike the emotional states included in the affect extended module, pain does not appear in the most commonly used mental health screening tools, making it less likely for the longer recall period to conflate this measure with mental health outcomes. Furthermore, this framing aligns with its use in other OECD surveys (van den Berg et al., 2024[45]), providing consistency across OECD recommendations and enabling the benchmarking of outcomes for patient populations participating in the PaRIS survey with population-level outcomes. Some national statistical offices and health agencies may already collect data on pain in health surveys, but it is still recommended to measure pain using the additional question in the subjective well-being core module. Health surveys frequently include questions on pain – often further disaggregating pain by type (back pain, neck pain, etc.) – as well as questions about the duration of pain (chronic pain measures) and the extent to which pain interferes with daily activities. For example, the European Health Interview survey includes a question asking respondents, "how much bodily pain have you had during the past 4 weeks?" These questions provide needed information about physical health, but they are conceptually different from a general question asking about a respondent's reported pain. At times, health surveys may include general questions on pain that do not specify "physical" pain. Additionally – while specific practice may vary across OECD countries – in general, health surveys are typically not fielded annually, as opposed to general social surveys; to monitor population pain prevalence and make meaningful comparisons between groups (and over time), frequent data collection is needed.

Affect balance vs. mental health screening tools

The first edition of the *Guidelines* included three affect questions in the core module (feeling happy, worried or depressed). The 2023 review of country uptake of those guidelines found that countries were collecting data on each of these states, showing that the *construct* had traction among data producers, whereas the *measures* used by data producers varied widely. Data producers often use mental health tools to collect this information – in part, no doubt, because many existing surveys (in particular health surveys) include mental health screening tools.

To mitigate the potential confusion between affect and mental health measures, the second edition of the *Guidelines* has taken a different approach:

- The series of affect questions asking respondents how they felt the day prior are not included in the core module. The sole affect question is a new measure on pain, given its policy relevance and lack of inclusion in leading mental health screening tools.
- Greater clarity is provided on what affect measures are capturing, as opposed to mental health measures, and how data producers and policy makers may want to use both (Box A A.1).
- The implementation details accompanying the affect extended module (Box 2.5) and population mental health module (Box 2.7) provide data producers with clear instructions on how to capture data for each.

Box A A.1. Affect vs. mental health: When to use each measurement approach

Affect refers to a person's feelings or emotional states, typically measured with reference to a particular point in time. Affect measures aim to capture feelings and emotional states *as they are experienced*, and not as they are *remembered*. For this reason, data on affective states should be measured as closely as possible to the reference period. The first edition of the *Guidelines* recommended using a "yesterday" framing, to minimise distance from the recall period and thus the associated recall bias. This approach works well for household surveys. However, affect data are also particularly valuable when included in time use surveys (see Box 2.8).

Data collected through affect measures can be reported as the share of the population experiencing each affective state the day prior. Another approach is to create an affect balance measure, which captures the net balance between positive and negative affect. Data producers can then report the share of the population with a net negative affect balance. Affect balance is a useful metric in that it acknowledges that it is normal, and even healthy, to experience negative emotions; what is deemed a negative overall outcome is when the negative emotions outweigh positive emotions, on average, for a population group. Affect balance also smooths out cultural and regional differences in the likelihood of reporting extreme emotions (both positive and negative), allowing for more meaningful cross-country comparisons.

Affect data have been used to help shape a range of policy interventions, including child-custody arrangements, physical health or healthcare needs (e.g. end-of-life care), transitory changes such as the impact of a cultural event or feelings while commuting, and to highlight affective trade-offs such as sacrificing enjoyment now for long-term goals considered worthwhile (Mahoney, 2023[3]). Furthermore, empirical research using data from national statistical offices has shown affect balance to be sensitive to mental health outcomes, social relationships and financial conditions, making it a meaningful and responsive way to explore inequalities (Pérez Amador, 2023[51]; Pérez Amador, 2025[52]).

While some mental health conditions have affective components (such as affective and anxiety disorders), *mental health* is a distinct concept much broader than the experience of a particular feeling or emotion. Per the WHO definition, mental health is a "state of mental well-being that enables people to cope with the stresses of life, realize their abilities, learn well and work well, and contribute to their community" (WHO, 2022[53]). Mental health comprises both mental ill-health and specific mental health conditions such as major depressive disorder or generalised anxiety disorder, as well as positive mental health. Nevertheless, common measurement instruments for assessing the latter can share several characteristics with positive affect measures. One distinction between measures used to assess mental health and those used to measure affect is the reference period typically adopted. Because affect measurement instruments are designed to measure *feelings as they are experienced*, reference periods are short and recent. Mental health tools, on the other hand, are designed to pick up on the persistence of emotions and moods over a longer period of time – usually over the past two or four weeks – which can suggest risk for a mental health condition, or in the case of a positive mental health tool, indicate a healthy mental state. Because mental health tools are designed and tested as a multi-item set, it is not recommended to report prevalence rates for individual items in the tool. Instead, mental health tools should be scored and reported on according to validated processes, which are outlined in detail in the implementation details that accompany the module.

Eudaimonic measurement in the core module

The core module retains the same eudaimonic measure that appeared in the first edition of the *Guidelines* – the extent to which respondents feel that the things they do in their lives are worthwhile. The initial 2023 scoping review (investigating up-take of the 2013 *Guidelines*) found only a small number of OECD national statistical offices had taken this construct on board in regular (e.g. annual) national surveys, which clarified the need for a better understanding of the policy relevance of this measure (Mahoney, 2023[3]).

A deep review of the literature on eudaimonia suggests that, given limited survey space, a single question on worth, meaning and purpose remains the most suitable single-item eudaimonic question for household surveys (Abdallah and Mahoney, 2024[12]). The reasons are three-fold. First, the construct appears in almost all of the leading theoretical models of eudaimonia (refer to Table 2.2 in (Abdallah and Mahoney, 2024[12])), providing grounds for its inclusion as a core component of what constitutes eudaimonic subjective well-being. The construct, then, is well founded in the theoretical literature. Additionally, measures of worth and meaning show discriminant validity from life satisfaction, suggesting the two capture distinct latent constructs, therefore strengthening the argument for including both in the core module (Kudrna et al., 2024[11]).

Second, a sense of worth, meaning and purpose in one's life is associated with many policy-relevant outcomes, especially in the health sphere. It is linked to long-term physical and mental health and is associated with reduced all-cause mortality (Joshanloo and Blasco-Belled, 2023[54]; Alimujiang et al., 2019[55]; Boyle et al., 2009[56]; Cohen, Bavishi and Rozanski, 2016[57]; Hill and Turiano, 2014[58]; Martela, Laitinen and Hakulinen, 2024[59]). A lowered sense of meaning is predictive of the onset of chronic conditions four years in the future (Steptoe and Fancourt, 2019[60]) and is associated with heart-related conditions (Cohen, Bavishi and Rozanski, 2016[57]; Kim et al., 2013[61]; Kim et al., 2013[62]), disrupted sleep (Kim, Hershner and Strecher, 2015[63]; Steptoe and Fancourt, 2019[60]), reduced physical functionality in older adult populations (Kim et al., 2017[64]; Steptoe and Fancourt, 2019[60]) and obesity (Steptoe and Fancourt, 2019[60]). Conversely, higher levels of worth, meaning and purpose are linked to a greater likelihood of using preventative healthcare services (Chen et al., 2019[65]; Kim, Strecher and Ryff, 2014[66]), engaging in more physical activity, better eating habits and lowered alcohol consumption (Steptoe and

Fancourt, 2019[60]). Beyond health, a sense of meaning in the workplace is associated with higher productivity (Martikainen et al., 2022[67]), and meaning and purpose are related to reduced risk of divorce and closer relationships with friends (Steptoe and Fancourt, 2019[60]) as well as with higher rates of volunteering (Chen et al., 2019[65]; Steptoe and Fancourt, 2019[60]). Meaning in life is also associated more broadly with prosocial behaviours (Steger et al., 2008[68]).

Finally, OECD scoping work in 2023 found that seven OECD countries were actively and regularly measuring a sense of meaning and purpose using the recommended measure (those countries are Canada, France, Korea, Mexico, New Zealand, Norway and the United Kingdom) (Mahoney, 2023[3]). Any changes to the wording of this question would disrupt time series in the countries that have been most active in measuring this construct (and in some cases, where those data have been contributing to the evidence base for the policy relevance of meaning (What Works Wellbeing, 2021[69])). Thus, there would need to be a compelling evidence-based rationale for changing the wording of the recommended question.

For these reasons, the original eudaimonia question is retained in this second edition of the *Guidelines*. It is understood that some official data producers had difficulty in translating this question into languages other than English (Abdallah and Mahoney, 2024[12]), as is evidenced by the findings of a 2013 Eurostat report on that year's European Union Statistics on Income and Living Conditions (EU-SILC) survey, which contained this question on things in life being worthwhile in its ad hoc well-being module (Eurostat, 2013[70]). In certain languages, the translation gave respondents the impression that the question was asking about accomplishments in their life (which can be associated with financial or labour market achievements) or the perceived futility of actions in life. Additional contextual information has been provided in the implementation details accompanying the core module, both to provide enumerators with the needed context to understand what this question is aiming to capture and to assist effective translations. The Mexican national statistical office provides an example of how translations of this question into the target language can effectively capture the intended meaning, even if the exact language used needs to be slightly amended: INEGI's translation to Spanish specifies "Por lo general, siento que lo que hago en mi vida vale la pena," a formulation that maintains the original meaning (the things one does in life are worthwhile) while using accessible and widely understood language in the Mexican context.

Changes made to extended modules

Information supporting the creation of extended modules is provided in the sections below. The largest change between the first and second edition of the *Guidelines* is the refinement of the composition of the extended modules and of the measures contained therein. While in the first edition of the *Guidelines* these modules provided a range of different tools that could be used to measure the same construct, in this edition the modules present a set of the most important constructs to measure within each component of subjective well-being, and a single measure is recommended for each construct. Care was also taken to understand whether the constructs are truly components of *subjective well-being*, or whether they are separate constructs measured elsewhere in the OECD Well-being Framework (Box A A.2). Whenever an extended module includes a measure that also appears in the core module, that measure is **bolded** to alert data producers to avoid double-collection.

Box A A.2. Social connections and subjective well-being

Relational measures are closely intertwined with subjective well-being measures, and measures of perceived isolation, loneliness and connection to others often appear in multi-item scales designed to capture psychological flourishing. Indeed, background research commissioned as part of the *Guidelines* update on how to measure affect and eudaimonia identified social and relational measures as being important constructs underpinning both (Kudrna et al., 2024[11]; Abdallah and Mahoney, 2024[12]). Additionally, two of the most widely used approaches to eudaimonic well-being measurement place relational well-being as a core component (Ryan and Deci, 2000[71]; Ryff, 1989[72]). Separately, the review of subjective well-being measurement tools from culturally and regionally diverse population groups – with a focus on Indigenous measurement approaches – also pulled up many examples of communal, social and relational measures (Smith et al., 2025[13]). Lastly, research led by OECD country national statistical offices highlights the strong interplay between social connections and subjective well-being. The Mexican ENBIARE 2025 well-being survey included a set of three items to assess the emotional reciprocity, respect and collaborative aspects of intimate relationships – covering the extent to which respondents (1) admire their partner's qualities, (2) feel their opinions are taken into account in decision-making, and (3) consider their relationship to function as a team. Outcomes from subsequent analysis of the survey by INEGI (the Mexican statistical office) revealed these measures of relationship quality to significantly enhance the explanatory power of models of subjective well-being.

It is clear that social interactions and close relationships with others are deeply important for overall well-being, and indeed the OECD Well-being Framework includes a dimension of social capital (containing measures of time spent with others, perceived social support, satisfaction with relationships and loneliness). However, what is less clear is the extent to which these measures enter into the previously established subjective well-being framework (Box 1.2) – are these constructs subjective well-being *outcomes*, or *determinants* of these outcomes?

Upcoming work at the OECD will produce separate measurement guidelines for social connections. That future activity will include developing a theoretical framework of the construct, identifying the components that should be measured – both objective aspects (e.g. time spent with others vs. time spent alone, network size and composition) and subjective (e.g. the perception that social needs are met, and measures of the quality of relationships and social interactions) – and propose a core module of recommended measures, identifying those with the strongest statistical properties to capture each policy-relevant construct. This work is on-going at the time of this publication.

While not synonymous with subjective well-being, aspects of social connections are deeply relevant to subjective well-being outcomes, and there are overlapping areas in the conceptual framing of both. This is in many ways not dissimilar to the relationship between subjective well-being and mental health measures: mental health is *not* synonymous with subjective well-being. However, mental health measures include questions assessing the affective states of respondents and in this way often overlap with some measures of subjective well-being. This edition of the *Guidelines* provides clarifying information on how to use and interpret affect vs. mental health measures to help data producers better understand the relationship between the two (Box A A.1).

When explicit OECD recommendations on social connections measurement are available, the OECD will provide data producers with similar guidance as to how they relate to existing subjective well-being measurement guidelines and how to incorporate the new social connections core module alongside subjective well-being modules. In the interim, data producers already collecting subjective data on social connections – including, but not limited to, measures capturing *perceived social support*, *loneliness* and *satisfaction with relationships* – can include these measures at the end of their subjective well-being survey module or position them immediately following the subjective well-being portion of the survey.

Life evaluation extended module

Life evaluation measures capture respondents' reflective assessments of their life overall, or of specific aspects of it (Diener, Lucas and Oishi, 2002[73]). Evaluative measures are subjective appraisals, rather than a description of an emotional state – the latter being a feature of affect measures. The process of making an evaluation may involve the respondent envisioning a standard outcome that they view as appropriate and then comparing their circumstances to that standard (Pavot et al., 1991[74]) – whether consciously or unconsciously.

The life evaluation extended module (Box 2.3) includes the primary measure of subjective well-being, the question on life satisfaction (Q1). Alternative approaches to measuring satisfaction with life, which had been included in this module in the first edition, have been removed in order to reduce redundancies and strengthen the OECD's recommended approach for measuring this construct. A question about perceived satisfaction with life in the past (Q2) has also been retained; however, it has been adapted to ask respondents how satisfied they were *one* year ago (instead of five years ago); having a more recent reference period decreases the cognitive burden on respondents. Such recalled measures of life satisfaction have value-add in that they are informative in understanding how to interpret current life satisfaction measures and the dynamics of life satisfaction in general (Prati and Senik, 2022[75]).

A new question on hope (Q3) has been added to the life evaluation module. Hope implies both a positive outlook towards the future as well as a sense of agency to achieve good outcomes. This is often differentiated from optimism, a personality trait associated with assuming the best – without an inherent sense of one's role in achieving good outcomes. This makes hope a more relevant outcome to capture, from a subjective well-being perspective (Abdallah and Mahoney, 2024[12]). Hope is associated with many other economic, relational and civic well-being outcomes. Lack of hope is associated with premature mortality (Graham and Pinto, 2019[76]; O'Connor and Graham, 2019[77]), while more hope can have health benefits in patient populations (Tremolada et al., 2020[78]; Snyder, 2000[79]). Hope is also associated with voting patterns (Ward, 2019[80]; Ward et al., 2021[81]), and lack of hope is possibly correlated with higher susceptibility to misinformation (Graham, 2024[82]). People who report higher levels of hope are more likely to invest in their future (Lybbert and Wydick, 2018[83]), including in their education (Graham and Pozuelo, 2023[84]), and they are more likely to engage in political activism and climate action (Leshem, 2019[85]; Cohen-Chen and Van Zomeren, 2018[86]; Klar and Kasser, 2009[87]; Geiger, Dwyer and Swim, 2023[88]). The psychometric properties of multi-item hope scales have been tested (Edwards et al., 2007[89]; Pleeging, 2022[90]); however, single-item measures are relatively new. The question introduced in the life evaluation extended module is used by the United Kingdom's Office for National Statistics (ONS) (ONS, 2024[91]) and underwent cognitive testing prior to its addition to official surveys and to the ONS's Well-being Database.

The domain evaluation extended module remains unchanged from the first edition of the *Guidelines*. Given the short length of the preceding life evaluation extended module, data producers who value domain satisfaction questions can easily combine elements of the two modules. It is acknowledged that there are domains of life not currently well represented by the extended module, and future iterations may explore these topics in greater depth once more evidence is available. As one example, rather than asking a question about job satisfaction, the Mexican statistical office (INEGI) includes a question in its 2025 ENBIARE well-being survey asking respondents, "How satisfied are you with your main activity (work, housework, studying, caring for or assisting a family member)." This formulation – using the term "main activity" rather than "job" – allows respondents to reflect on both paid and unpaid work, making the question applicable to a broader share of the population.

Affect extended module

Affect measures capture information about feelings and emotional states as people experience them, or as close to the time as possible, rather than evaluative measures of feelings in general (see Box A A.1 for more details). Affect measures usually are composed of a battery of measures asking respondents their experience of a list of different emotional states. There are different theoretical approaches to affect measurement to structure which emotions are selected for inclusion (see (Kudrna et al., 2024[11]) for a brief overview). The circumplex model of affect captures the multidimensionality of affect by plotting two dimensions of classification: positive vs. negative emotions and low vs. high arousal. This theoretical model provides the underpinning for the selection of the four short-list measures of affect in the extended affect module (Box 2.5).

As is illustrated in Figure A A.1, the four affect measures making up the short list of measures (in case of limited survey space) cover each of the four quadrants: high-arousal negative affect (worried), high-arousal positive affect (happy), low-arousal negative affect (sad) and low-arousal positive affect (calm). Having two positive and two negative affective states allows for the calculation of an evenly balanced affect balance. This recommendation deviates only slightly from the short list of affect measures in the first edition of the *Guidelines*. First, the new set measures "sad" rather than "depression", electing to measure mental health states using mental health tools (see Box A A.1 and Box 2.7). The second change is the addition of calm. Based on research suggesting that negative affect is more multidimensional than positive affect, the first edition of the *Guidelines* elected to include a single positive affect measure (happy) in its short set of affect measures. A recent review of the literature finds that affective measures of calm and peace show greater discriminant validity from life satisfaction than do measures of happiness – illustrating that calm vs. happy are capturing different latent constructs (Kudrna et al., 2024[11]). Separately, a review of globally inclusive approaches to subjective well-being measurement highlights that, despite the importance given to low arousal positive emotions in Eastern philosophy and traditions like Confucianism, Taoism and Buddhism, the value of the emotion is universal (Smith et al., 2025[13]). Findings from the Gallup World Poll support the global relevance of feeling calm, showing that it is both experienced and valued by populations worldwide and not centred on a specific geographic region (Lomas et al., 2022[92]).

Figure A A.1. Circumplex model of affect

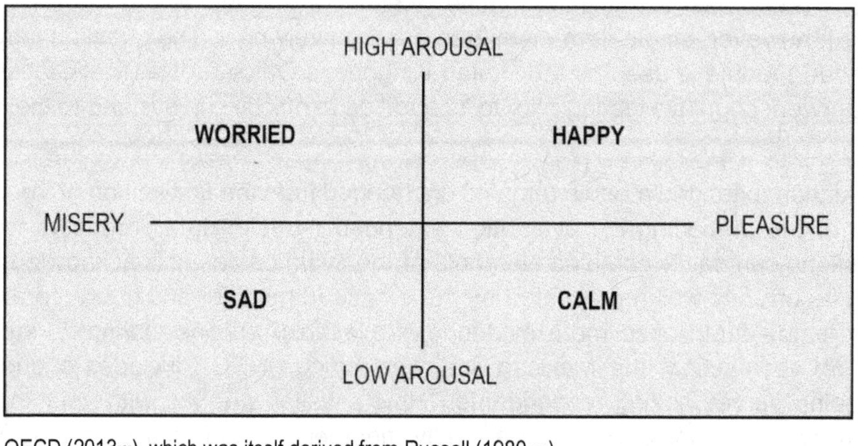

Source: Adapted from OECD (2013[2]), which was itself derived from Russell (1980[93]).

The remaining measures in the affect extended module comprise a long list of affect measures, which data producers can field if they have sufficient space. These measures are retained from the first edition, with a few minor adjustments. The question on "enjoyment" has been changed to "joyful", based on findings from Kudrna et al. (2024[11]).

Eudaimonia extended module

A core research question for updating the guidelines was a better understanding of eudaimonia, by distilling lessons from its vast multi-disciplinary literature. A recent working paper review of the most prominent theoretical frameworks of eudaimonia finds that, in its essence, eudaimonia is about a sense of living well (Abdallah and Mahoney, 2024[12]). This constitutes: (1) motivations (orientations, attitudes or values that determine behaviour), (2) feelings (emotional states) and (3) behaviours (observable actions). *Eudaimonia*, then, can be defined as an orientation towards feelings that value, and actions that foster, a long-term positive impact on oneself and others. In the context of measuring subjective well-being (which is specifically about the mental states that people experience, rather than their behaviours), it is the *feelings* component that is of greatest relevance – and *eudaimonic feelings* can be understood as the set of universally desirable feelings or experiences associated with a sense of living well. Both definitions imply a multidimensional concept, with different constructs that should be captured in an extended eudaimonia measurement module (Abdallah and Mahoney, 2024[12]).

To refine the list of constructs that should be measured, the same working paper applied the following criteria: the construct is included in the existing academic literature; it fits well under the working definition of eudaimonia; it has predictive power for policy-relevant outcomes; it is distinct from life satisfaction and therefore not duplicative; and, lastly, that there are existing measures (preferably in official statistics) to measure the construct (Abdallah and Mahoney, 2024[12]). This yielded a list of the following constructs, all of which are included in the eudaimonia extended module (Box 2.6):

- The things one does in life are worthwhile (Q1) – as in the core module
- Autonomy (Q2)
- Competence, accomplishment or environmental mastery (Q3)
- Self-esteem or self-acceptance (Q4)
- Personal growth and self-actualisation (Q5).

The working paper highlighted additional constructs that are not included in the extended module for space reasons; only the top-performing constructs were selected for inclusion. The one exception is the construct of relatedness. This construct performed well on the six selection criteria, but it is a measure of social connection and therefore is not included in these recommendations (see Box A A.2 for a discussion on the relationship between subjective well-being and social connections and on forthcoming measurement guidance on social connections).

Of the selected measures, three were consistent with the first edition of the *Guidelines*: Q1 (worth / meaning), Q3 (competence) and Q4 (self-esteem). For Q2, while the construct of autonomy was retained, the question used has been updated. The new measure was developed by Martela and Ryan as a validated single-item assessment of the construct of autonomy (2024[94]), and it was fielded by the Finnish Prime Minister's Office via its Citizens' Pulse survey from 2022-2024 (Statistics Finland, 2024[95]). It will be included in the forthcoming European Social Survey 2025 well-being module, where cognitive testing in advance of fielding the full survey has found that it performs well (Rutherford et al., 2024[96]).

The eudaimonia module contains one new measure, on personal growth (Q5). Unlike other measures of eudaimonia, personal growth is future-oriented and contributes to the sustainability of subjective well-being into the future – this makes it an important conceptual addition to the module. Personal growth has been found to be associated with improved physical health outcomes (e.g. metabolic syndrome) (Ryff, Boylan and Kirsch, 2021[97]). Measures on personal growth have been assessed as a part of longer scales on eudaimonic or psychological well-being (Ryff and Keyes, 1995[98]; Waterman et al., 2010[99]) that use an agree/disagree formulation (often with Likert scale responses). The measure included in the eudaimonia module is a single item taken from Ryff's Psychological Well-being Scale (Ryff and Keyes, 1995[98]; Ryff,

2014[100]), which itself (as a whole) has been extensively validated, translated into 40+ languages and integrated into a large-scale nationally-representative longitudinal survey (UW Madison, 2025[101]).

Mental health module

A module on population mental health measures is included in this edition of the *Guidelines* to provide data producers with clarity as to how mental health measurement approaches can complement subjective well-being measures, and more specifically, how mental health measures differ in their implementation and subsequent interpretation from affect measures (see Box A A.1).

The recommendations in the mental health extended module pull from previous OECD work, in particular *Measuring Population Mental Health* (OECD, 2023[102]). This publication was the first in a series of two: the second, *How to Make Societies Thrive? Coordinating Approaches to Promote Well-being and Mental Health* (OECD, 2023[103]), looks at the policy implications of the wide-ranging societal impacts of mental health outcomes. Interested readers can reference that original report for greater detail on conceptual frameworks for mental health measurement, an overview of OECD national statistics offices' current practice, and methodological and measurement considerations. This deep review culminated in the three recommendations included in the extended module: a general self-assessment of one's mental health; the four-item Patient Health Questionnaire to assess the risk of depression and anxiety; and the five-item WHO-5 Well-being Index to measure positive mental health. The mental ill-health measure suggested also aligns with on-going pilot data collection work undertaken by the OECD Health Division to measure the performance of mental health systems. In that stream of work, the full-length, eight-item Patient Health Questionnaire (PHQ-8) is recommended to measure risk for depression, and the full-length seven-item Generalized Anxiety Disorder (GAD-7) survey is recommended to measure risk for anxiety (OECD, forthcoming[104]).

Time use modules

Time use surveys are especially suitable for the collection of affect measures, because by integrating these measures into time use diaries, it is possible to capture people's emotional experiences *as they happen* (or close to it) – tied to specific activities – rather than *as they are recalled*. Affective states should be measured, because they can be used to assess policy impacts in specific cases where general life evaluation measures may be less pertinent (refer to Box A A.1 for a brief list).

Affect data that capture how people are feeling in the moment is particularly useful when that information is tied to the activities the person is engaging in *while* feeling that way and to whom they are with. These data have direct policy applications, for example, understanding the full cost associated with sitting in traffic during commuting time (which can then inform congestion pricing policy) (Krekel and MacKerron, 2023[105]); providing new methodologies for valuing the benefits of green spaces (Smith, 2023[106]); or better crafting labour market or workplace well-being interventions (Mylona, 2023[107]; Krueger and Mueller, 2012[108]; Hoang and Knabe, 2021[109]; Wolf et al., 2019[110]). International guidance on time use surveys is now highlighting the important role of such data in understanding (gender) patterns in unpaid work and caregiving (UNSD, 2025[111]; Tchipeva, Miceli and Ninka, 2024[112]). Integrating affect questions into these time use diaries would help more fully capture the cognitive burden of these tasks and provide a comprehensive view of how people value their time (Krekel and MacKerron, 2023[113]). Lastly, the social aspect of time use surveys (asking respondents whom they were with during each activity) provides insight into the dynamics of spending time with others in person and our emotional states, as well as the association between engaging in certain activities – such as the use of digital technologies – and feelings of loneliness and disconnection (OECD, 2025[114]).

Experience sampling

Experience sampling methods involve collecting data on affective states in real time. There are different ways to approach data collection, and increasingly smartphone-based surveys are being used. As one example, in 2021 Statistics Canada piloted an experience sampling survey, the Pilot Study on Everyday Well-being. The survey used an app to field questions about affective states up to five times a day, over a thirty-day period. During each check-in, respondents were asked how happy, anxious, relaxed, focused or in control of their emotions they felt (Figure A A.2). The survey was designed in collaboration with the Canada Council for the Arts and Canadian Heritage to focus on the impact of the arts and cultural activities on overall well-being (Kudrna et al., 2024[11]).

Figure A A.2. Experience sampling methodology example from Statistics Canada

Pilot Study on Everyday Well-being (CAN)

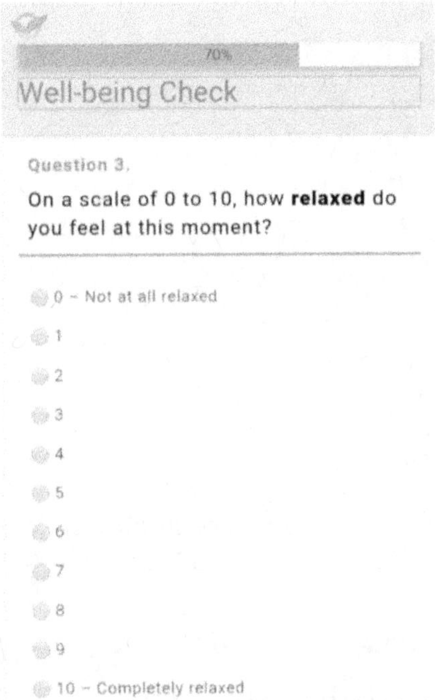

Source: Kudrna et al. (2024[11]), "Measuring affective components of subjective well-being: Updated evidence to inform national data collections", *OECD Papers on Well-being and Inequalities*, No. 31, OECD Publishing, Paris, https://doi.org/10.1787/6c72da70-en.

Full day time use diary method

The full day time use diary method module (Box 2.8) provides a means of integrating affect data in time use diaries; this approach has been implemented by a number of OECD national statistical offices. For example, this approach has been used by INSEE, the French statistical agency, in its time use survey, Enquête Emploi du temps 2010; the Italian statistical agency, Istat, has also used this approach in its last two full-length time use surveys (see Figure A A.3, Panel A for the 2023 questionnaire). Both the French and Italian measures use the same answer scale (from -3 (very unpleasant) to +3 (very pleasant)), with varying reports of its efficacy. Istat has found the answer scale to be effective and plans to continue using it in 2033, when the next time use survey is fielded. INSEE, on the other hand, will change its approach in the 2025-26 time use survey and will instead field a series of measures on general satisfaction with time use (see below for more details). Statistics Finland has fielded a variation of this approach but uses a visual approach rather than a numeric scale (the faces are coded +2, +1, 0, -1, -2, respectively, when interpreting the data – see Figure A A.3, Panel B). Another answer scale variation is that used by Statistics Canada in its time use surveys: respondents are asked, "On a scale of 1 to 5 where 1 means "Very unpleasant" and 5 means "Very pleasant", how would you rate the activity you were doing?" (Statistics Canada, 2022[115]).

Figure A A.3. Full day time use diary examples from Italy and Finland

Panel A. Indagine statistica multiscoppo sulle famiglie (ITA)

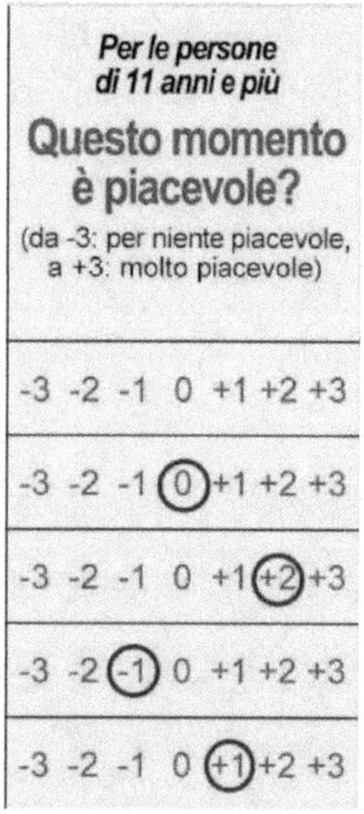

Panel B. Statistics Finland (FIN)

Source: Panel A: Istat (2023[116]), *Como uso il mio tempo: Indagine statistica multiscoppo sulle famiglie*, https://siqual.istat.it/SIQual/files/IMF-13%20B%20Anno%202022-23.pdf?ind=0071301&cod=5591&progr=1&tipo=4. Panel B: Statistics Finland.

Random sample of three activities within a time use diary

One alternative to gathering affect data for every activity experienced in a time use diary is to ask respondents a richer set of questions about a random sub-set of just three activities (episodes) only. By reducing the number of activities assessed, it is possible to expand the question set to include multiple positive and negative affective states, for example, how happy, worried, calm, sad, lonely or in pain the respondent felt, or how meaningful the activity was. This approach follows a format similar to the Princeton Affect and Time Survey (Krueger et al., 2009[117]), and it has been adopted by the American Time Use Survey (ATUS), which administered a well-being module in 2010, 2012-13 and most recently in 2021 (Figure A A.4).

This type of data collection may be prioritised over the full day diary where the need for data on several separate affective states (e.g. in a medical study where separate information about pain and tiredness may be paramount) takes priority over the goal of calculating an accurate daily affect measure for each individual respondent. Thus, the data collection method to prioritise depends on the research goal.

This approach is typically administered in an interview shortly following the completion of a time use diary. Because recall is important, it is desirable that the interview take place as soon as possible after the diary has been completed – preferably the day after the day covered by the diary. Three episodes are selected from the time use diary, omitting episodes when the respondent was sleeping or otherwise unconscious.

The procedure is designed to select episodes ensuring that, over the sample as a whole, there are an adequate number of responses for each major time use activity. Because of the complexity of the sampling design, it is important to weight responses correctly to ensure that the resulting estimates are representative (refer to (BLS, 2022[118]) for a detailed discussion). The module randomly selects three activities from a time use diary and asks respondents how happy, tired, stressed, sad or in pain they felt during the episode (for example), as well as the extent to which they found the activity meaningful. Figure A A.4 shows an example of what this module looks like using the Web CATI instrument interface.

Figure A A.4. Example abbreviated day reconstruction diary module: American Time Use Survey

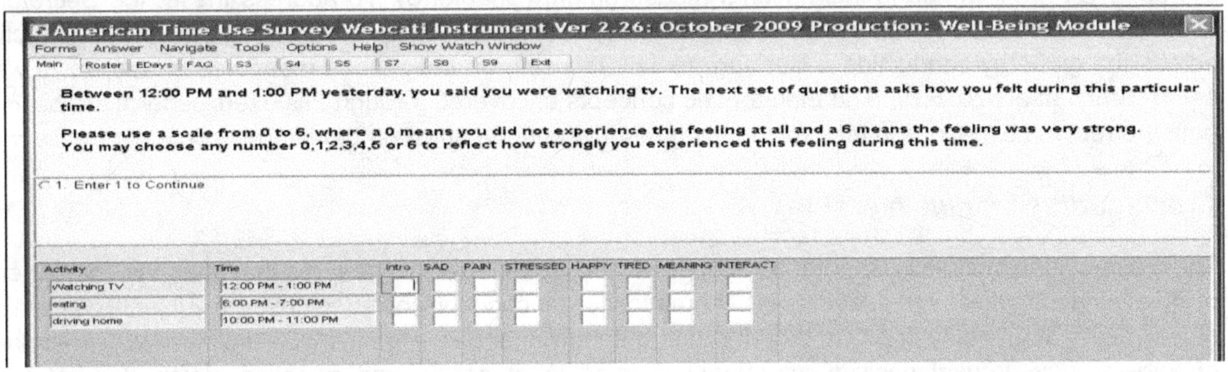

Source: Kudrna et al. (2024[11]), "Measuring affective components of subjective well-being: Updated evidence to inform national data collections", *OECD Papers on Well-being and Inequalities*, No. 31, OECD Publishing, Paris, https://doi.org/10.1787/6c72da70-en.

General assessments of satisfaction with time use

Other general evaluations and assessments of one's time use have been included in time use surveys fielded by national statistical offices as a means of incorporating subjective assessments of time use. These questions can be implemented alongside the day reconstruction method outlined in Box 2.8, by asking respondents general questions upon completion of the time use diary. Examples include:

- Overall, how satisfied are you with how you use your time? [0-10] (Adapted from a question that appears in Statistics Canada's *2022 Time Use Survey* (Statistics Canada, 2022[115]).)
- Overall, how satisfied are you with the balance between your job and home life? [0-10] (Adapted from a question that appears in Statistics Canada's *2022 Time Use Survey* (Statistics Canada, 2022[115]).)
- Overall, how satisfied are you with the division of the housekeeping burden between you and your partner? [0-10] (Adapted from INSEE's *2025-26 Time Use Survey*.)
- Overall, how satisfied are you with the division of family care duties between you and your partner? [0-10] (Adapted from INSEE's *2025-26 Time Use Survey*.)
- A series of questions included in Eurostat's *2020 Harmonised European Time Use Surveys Guidelines* (Eurostat, 2020[119]), immediately following the time use diary portion:
    - What was the most pleasant activity described in the diary?
    - What was the most unpleasant activity described in the diary?
    - What was the most stressful activity described in the diary?
    - Overall, how do you appreciate this day?
    - (These questions do not directly capture affect, in that they are evaluative and prime the respondent to think in comparative terms rather than focusing on states, moods or emotions

that are experienced in the moment. They are therefore not recommended for understanding subjective well-being outcomes but can be used for other purposes.)

Cross-cutting experimental module and question banks

The experimental measures and concepts included in Chapter 3's cross-cutting module reflect findings motivated by one of the three research streams underpinning this guidelines update: exploring globally inclusive approaches to subjective well-being measurement to ensure the broad relevance of OECD recommendations (covered by the resulting modules in Chapter 2) and to identify important concepts that are as-of-yet not included in international measurement (Chapter 3). To address these, the Secretariat commissioned a working paper that, among other issues, explored the diversity of measurement practice across the globe by conducting a literature review focusing on Indigenous measures of subjective well-being (Smith et al., 2025[13]). The themes and concepts uncovered through this exercise form the basis of both the recommendations in the cross-cutting module and the question banks that follow.

Cross-cutting module measures

The cross-cutting module in Chapter 3 includes subjective well-being measures that span the components of life evaluation, affect and eudaimonia. Thematically, the concepts included cover: a subjective appraisal of well-being of an entity or group broader than the individual (Q1 – family; Q3 – spirituality; Q4 – impact on others); low-arousal positive affect (Q2 – mind is at ease); and affective states that relate to interpersonal interactions (Q5 – treated with respect; Q6 – envious; Q7 – compassionate; Q8 – forgiving; Q9 – fearful; Q10 – generous; Q11 – selfish) (Box 3.1).

The first question in the module asks respondents to reflect on how well they perceive their family to be doing these days. The question comes from the New Zealand General Social Survey (GSS), a biennial population-wide data collection exercise (Statistics New Zealand, 2023[120]). It was adapted for the GSS from Te Kupenga – a survey designed to capture the social, cultural and economic well-being of the Māori from their cultural perspective (Statistics New Zealand, 2014[121]). Respondents are not prompted as to what constitutes "family"; in the original New Zealand questionnaire, a follow-up question asks respondents to clarify which group(s) of people they included in their consideration of family, from the following list:

- Parents, spouse / partner, siblings, children, brothers /sisters and/or parents-in-law
- Grandparents, grandchildren
- Aunts / uncles, cousins, nephews / nieces, other in-laws
- Close friends, others

This allows for a broad and non-prescriptive understanding of family. Family well-being is a broadly relevant concept; though the question was initially developed for the Māori population (the original question wording asking how one's whānau is doing – a Māori term that loosely translates to family but has a broader implication), it has performed well since its inclusion in the population-wide New Zealand General Social Survey. Analytical work on this measure suggests that, while highly correlated with life satisfaction, it is distinct, especially in its drivers: an individual's own health and material well-being are stronger determinants of their life satisfaction than they are of how well their family is doing (Smith, Peach and Cording, 2019[122]). Beyond New Zealand, a study in the United States found that the well-being of the respondent's family ranked highly in a discrete choice experiment ranking the most important aspects of one's well-being (Benjamin et al., 2014[123]). Evaluations of family, communal and interpersonal well-being appear in the vast majority of Indigenous subjective well-being measurement tools (Smith et al., 2025[13]).

The second question is a low-arousal positive affect measure (recall the circumplex model of affect, shown in Figure A A.1) asking respondents how often their mind is at ease. This question comes from the Gallup-WPE Global Wellbeing Initiative, which has been fielding questions in the annual Gallup World Poll since 2020. This specific question was included in the 2022 and 2023 iterations. This provides another dimension of low-arousal positive affect, distinct from calm (Box 2.5). In its field testing, Gallup found that other low-arousal positive affect states were difficult to translate: for example, a question on how "content" respondents felt was poorly understood (Lomas et al., 2022[124]). This question, then, provides an effective alternative.

The third question is a broadly framed, inclusive question about spirituality. Spirituality and the vibrancy of one's life is an important component of many Indigenous well-being approaches (Smith et al., 2025[13]), but it has broader relevance. There are strands of literature investigating different definitions of spirituality (Peng-Keller, 2019[125]; Hill et al., 2000[126]) and how it relates to subjective well-being (Ryff, 2021[127]; van Dierendonck, 2012[128]), which are developing an understanding of how spirituality fosters resilience and leads to better well-being outcomes broadly defined (Koenig, McCullough and Larson, 2001[129]; Long et al., 2024[130]). A range of different multi-item measurement scales have been developed – for an overview, see (Bohlmeijer et al., 2023[131]) – and the Harvard University Human Flourishing Program has curated a set of resources through its Spirituality & Flourishing working group (Human Flourishing Program, 2024[132]). Some existing subjective well-being measurement approaches include a spiritual dimension – for example, the Personal Wellbeing Index, included in the domain evaluation extended module (Box 2.4), includes an additional, optional question on spirituality: How satisfied are you with your spirituality or religion? (International Wellbeing Group, 2024[133]). The question in the experimental module pulls from the Spiritual Well-Being: The Awe Index scale (Hamby, Grych and Banyard, 2013[134]).

The fourth question, on beneficence, captures outcomes related to pro-social behaviours – improving outcomes not only for oneself, but for others around them. The pro-social behaviours themselves (e.g. volunteering, providing support to others) are measured in other domains of the OECD Well-being Framework, but measures capturing *beneficence* are not widely measured, and only a few studies have tested the psychometric properties of beneficence scales (Martela and Ryan, 2016[135]; Martela and Ryan, 2020[136]). Longer item scales measuring flourishing or psychological well-being contain measures that capture positive social relationships – which may also capture aspects of beneficence (Ryff and Keyes, 1995[98]; Diener et al., 2009[137]) – even though they have not been designed (nor tested) to do so directly. The measure in the module comes from a single item in a scale developed by Martela and Ryan (Martela and Ryan, 2016[135]), with the answer scale adapted to a 0-10 format to align with the rest of the module.

The final set of questions refer to relational affect questions – these are emotional experiences that are inherently social in that the emotion can be interpreted only in the context of other people or interpersonal interactions (Smith et al., 2025[13]). In case of limited space, three questions are prioritised (treated with respect, envious and compassionate), but the full set can be implemented should time and resources allow. These questions come from the Bhutan Gross National Happiness Survey (Ura et al., 2022[138]), with answer scales adapted to a 0-10 format to align with the rest of the module. Additionally, the questions have been slightly reworded to align with the rest of the module as well as with the affect extended module question framing (Box 2.5); similarly, a yesterday recall period is used. The Bhutan Gross National Happiness Survey collects data on the nine domains and 33 measures that make up the Gross National Happiness (GNH) Index, calculated every five years to assess overall well-being and happiness in the population (CBS, 2024[139]; OECD, 2024[140]).

Q5 is based on an existing question in the Gallup World Poll, asking respondents the extent to which they felt respected the day prior. (A question about feeling respected also appears in the Bhutan Gross National Happiness Survey.) The measure included in Box 3.1 is slightly adapted from the Gallup World Poll to have the answer scale match the rest of the measures in the module. This question has been translated into many languages and fielded in many countries worldwide. Gallup includes "respect" in its annual

Global Emotions reports (Gallup World Poll, 2024[141]). Respect and human dignity are fundamental to human rights (UN, 1948[142]; European Union Agency for Fundamental Rights, 2007[143]; UN, 2015[144]), and the effects of their absence has informed OECD work in understanding the detrimental impacts of discrimination (Hardy and Schraepen, 2024[145]).

Question banks

The scoping review pulled up additional themes that are broadly important for populations globally; however, these concepts were not able to be integrated into the cross-cutting experimental module, because there is not yet sufficient evidence to identify a well-performing, single-item measure to adequately capture the underlying construct. Because these concepts are important, and the evidence base should be expanded – which is possible only through the testing of new measures – question banks are provided with established examples from the literature. Data producers are encouraged to select from these options, balancing the needs of their local context and the purpose of the specific survey.

The first of these concepts is *balance and harmony*, which has been the focus of extensive field testing by the Gallup-WPE Global Wellbeing Initiative. Part of this process has been to unpack the conceptual differences between the two constructs. Lomas et al. (2022, p. 4[146]) put forward the following definitions:

- *Balance*: "the various elements which constitute a phenomenon, and/or the various forces acting upon it, are in proportionality and/or equilibrium, often with an implication of stability, evenness, and poise".
- *Harmony*: "various elements which constitute a phenomenon, and/or the various forces acting upon it, cohere and complement one another, leading to an overall configuration which is appraised positively".

The definitions are caveated with a statement that there is a strong connection between the two concepts, but note that harmony is more unambiguously positive and has a "warmer" feel to it (Lomas et al., 2022[146]; Abdallah and Mahoney, 2024[12]). Recent work has further examined this relationship and found that while respondents assessed harmony to be more positively valenced, they self-reported a preference for balance (Lomas et al., 2025[147]). What is clear, however, is that both concepts have been absent from most academic considerations of subjective well-being, in particular those developed in a Western context (Lomas et al., 2022[146]; Abdallah and Mahoney, 2024[12]) – this, despite the fact that an international study found that the most prominent definition of happiness included concepts of "inner harmony", which itself includes themes of inner peace, contentment and balance (Fave et al., 2016[148]; Smith et al., 2025[13]).

Results from Gallup's fielding of different measures capturing either balance or harmony have found them to be only somewhat correlated with life evaluation measures, showing value-add in comparison to life satisfaction (Lomas et al., 2022[92]; Kudrna et al., 2024[11]). However, cognitive testing of individual measures has illustrated the difficulties in translating specific question wording across linguistic and cultural groups. For example, here are field testing notes relating to issues with the question, "In general, how often are the various aspects of your life in balance?" (Lomas et al., 2022, p. 7[146]):

> *In cognitive interviews, respondents generally understood it, though interpreted "in balance" differently. About half of interviewees understood it to mean having enough time to spend on all things in life that are most important to them (including work, social relations, family, health, economy, food, and emotional aspects). Some respondents in Italy specifically said balance means "Everything is in its place and having enough time for oneself and for others," with one person saying balance means "having moments to relax from work." However, several respondents mentioned that "in balance" referred to a balance of good things and bad things in a person's life. Others spoke of resilience and achieving goals as being "in balance." Somewhat differently, a Japanese respondent said, ""I think 'in balance' means no bias. There is no bias in thinking or in daily life." The broad nature of the phrase "various aspects of your life" was also difficult for some respondents. For instance, for some respondents in Lebanon, issues such as violence, strikes, civil unrest, and instability in their*

country were considered to be among the "various aspects" of their lives, and thus their answers were influenced strongly by the present situation there.

An alternative question, "In general, how often are your thoughts and feelings in harmony?" was deemed difficult to understand and answer by members of this project's informal advisory group. Because the concepts of balance and harmony have demonstrated importance and relevance, it is hoped that the inclusion of multiple measurement tools will encourage data producers to experiment with the best formulation of the question to move towards a recommended measure in future.

The second concept with an associated question bank is *connection to future generations*. Many OECD countries have introduced legislation or national strategies that emphasise the importance of better managing economic, social and environmental assets to safeguard well-being for future generations (OECD, 2023[149]). Concepts of intergenerational well-being and a sense of connection to one's ancestors and descendants also feature prominently in many Indigenous worldviews and non-Western literature on subjective well-being, including, for example (Smith et al., 2025[13]):

The concern for the well-being of future generations features in many Indigenous cultures, such as the Seventh Generation Principle in Haudenosaunee philosophy and practices (Clarkson, Morrissette and Regallet, 2001[150]), the Māori notion of being a "good ancestor", the importance of "Caring for Country" in Australian Aboriginal culture, the principle of "malama aina" in Hawaiian culture, and the concept of "mino-bimaadiziwin" in Anishinaabe culture in North America, which means "the good life" or "continuous rebirth and renewal".

Despite this, few explicit measures exist to measure the concept. Known existing measures are included in this question box in order to encourage experimentation.

The final concept is *connection to nature*. There is a vast literature highlighting the importance of the natural world for subjective well-being and good physical and mental health outcomes (OECD, 2023[103]), most of which views the natural environment as a separate outcome from – and distinct driver of – subjective well-being. A review of Indigenous subjective well-being measurement approaches, however, highlights that nature is not always viewed as a distinct and separate entity – measures instead focus on interconnection or harmony with nature (Smith et al., 2025[13]):

In Andean Indigenous cultures (South America), the principle of "sumaq kawsay" (Quechua) or "buen vivir" (Spanish) is a holistic approach to life that emphasises harmony with nature, community well-being and sustainability. This philosophy includes the responsibility to maintain a healthy environment for future generations.

In Bhutan, the term "happiness" as used in the Gross National Happiness framework is seen as a relational construct – emphasising responsibility, harmony with nature and concern for the happiness of others (Ura, Alkire and Zangmo, 2012[151]).

This work has also been done in Western contexts, exploring how connection to nature feeds into concepts of eudaimonia and subjective well-being (Ryff, 2021[127]; Pritchard et al., 2020[152]; Richardson et al., 2021[153]). Indeed, there are a number of multi-item scales that have been designed to measure connection to nature (Salazar, Kunkle and Monroe, 2020[154]) – however, many were developed in the English-language context, and, as of yet, there are few single-item measures that have been validated. Furthermore, many of these scales are designed to be a measure people's value systems as they relate to nature, rather than a measure of subjective well-being that encompasses nature. The options in the question bank provide data producers with a starting point of options to explore this concept further.

Collecting subjective well-being data in minority populations

The above findings exploring globally inclusive approaches to subjective well-being measurement have centred on what has been learned in terms of broad-based relevance for measuring subjective well-being across populations and contexts. This enables official data producers from all OECD countries, regardless of geographic region or linguistic tradition, to identify important measurement concepts for further exploration.

However, the process of reviewing these concepts entailed surveying measurement tools and well-being frameworks that were developed by, or in conjunction with, Indigenous and minority communities. Data producers in OECD countries have developed surveys to measure outcomes in specific communities: New Zealand's Te Kupenga survey of the Māori population being just one example (Statistics New Zealand, 2014[121]). To help data producers understand the unique challenges and considerations of collaborating with minority populations when collecting subjective well-being data, a set of four good practices are described in Box A A.3.

Box A A.3. Collecting subjective well-being measures for minority populations

When collecting subjective well-being measures for Indigenous and minority populations, process matters. While the terms "minority" and "Indigenous" refer to distinct and diverse groups, both groups are frequently subjected to systemic discrimination (United Nations, 2018[155]) and share common experiences of marginalisation experiences (Kipuri, 2009[156]; McClintock, Mellsop and Kingi, 2011[157]; Tuhiwai Smith, 2021[158]). For Indigenous peoples, these experiences are rooted in historical colonisation, whereas other groups experience oppression due to discrimination based on their ethnicity, religion or language (United Nations, 2023[159]).

It is important to note that the terms "Indigenous" and "minority" encompass diverse populations, each with their own languages, cultures and customs. Both minority and Indigenous peoples have had their data and knowledge exploited in the name of research, creating intergenerational distrust that is still prevalent today. Data collection involving minority or Indigenous peoples must therefore be approached with humility, sensitivity and cultural competence (Ringelheim, 2008[160]; Tuhiwai Smith, 2021[158]).

Guiding principles for collecting subjective well-being measures for minority populations focus on 1) fostering community involvement; 2) taking a strengths-based approach; 3) developing local ethical guidelines; and 4) ensuring data sovereignty.

1. Fostering community involvement

Building relationships and trust with the community involved is critical to collecting data from minority and Indigenous populations. These relationships must be approached with humility and the willingness to collaborate on data collection, analysis and dissemination methods. Participatory research methodologies are often recommended when working with minority and Indigenous groups. These approaches empower and emphasise community voices (Datta, 2023[161]). Prioritising engagement processes, including consultations with trusted community organisations, elders, advisory committees and researchers, can help ensure practices that reflect community values (Fernandez et al., 2017[162]; Griffiths et al., 2021[163]). One way to do this can be to work with community members to co-develop a survey; such was the approach taken in creating the Survey of Living Conditions in the Arctic (Kruse et al., 2008[164]; Wu, 2021[165]).

Effective community engagement can be time-consuming. This is because effective community engagement often requires ongoing interaction beyond the data collection period. Participatory methods can also demand significant time commitments by participants, and a high respondent burden, particularly when there is a lack of trust or rapport between the researcher and the community (Datta, 2023[161]; De Las Nueces et al., 2012[166]). It is important to dedicate sufficient time and resources for this engagement process, which can only move at the speed of trust.

2. Taking a strengths-based approach

Too often, well-being in minority or Indigenous communities has been portrayed in a negative light, using well-being indicators that reflect the values of Western cultures (e.g. focusing on individual achievement). When applied to non-Western communities, these indicators can result in misleading conclusions, because they overlook or devalue aspects of well-being that are important in other cultural contexts, such as communal relationships, connection to land, spirituality and cultural vitality. Instead, a strengths-based approach to conceptualising and measuring well-being focuses on the resilience, capabilities and assets of communities rather than on deficits, problems or vulnerabilities. Taking a strengths-based approach empowers community members to recognise and build on their capacities and strengths to improve well-being. This fosters a sense of ownership and agency, encouraging active participation and engagement, which can lead to more sustainable and meaningful improvements in well-being.

3. Developing local ethical research guidelines

Where specific local ethical research guidelines exist, adherence to them is important to ensure that research practices are not only scientifically sound but also culturally appropriate and equitable, fostering mutual trust between researchers and the community. For example, the Good Spirit, Good Life measurement instrument was developed after approval by the Aboriginal Health Ethics Committee in Australia. In the absence of such guidelines, approval from key community representatives is crucial. This is seen in the development of a well-being questionnaire for On Reserve First Nation Peoples in Ontario and British Columbia, Canada, where approval was granted from the Chief's representatives of each First Nation community involved alongside the general ethical approval (Kant et al., 2014[167]). What might be considered ethical in one country or community could be seen as intrusive, offensive or harmful in another. For example, attitudes towards privacy, informed consent or the role of community leaders in decision-making can vary greatly. Institutional ethical review typically reflects Western practices and values. Where possible, local ethical guidelines reflecting community values and worldviews should be followed and reviewed by appropriate advisory boards (Griffiths et al., 2021[163]).

4. Ensuring data sovereignty

Data sovereignty plays a central role when collecting data with minority and Indigenous communities. Indigenous Data Sovereignty refers to the right of Indigenous people to have ownership over their data. This supports the self-determination of Indigenous peoples to govern their data and autonomously make decisions about the methods, management of data collection and its dissemination of (McClintock et al., 2021[168]). Although some Indigenous groups have data sovereignty guidelines, this is not currently the case for many minority groups. In these settings, there is a need to engage with the community to consider management principles for the data collected (Griffiths et al., 2021[163]; Ringelheim, 2008[160]).

Source: Taken from Smith, C. et al. (2025[13]), "Globally inclusive measures of subjective wellbeing: Updated evidence to inform national data collections".

References

Abdallah, S. and J. Mahoney (2024), "Measuring eudaimonic components of subjective well-being: Updated evidence to inform national data collections", *OECD Papers on Well-being and Inequalities*, No. 30, OECD Publishing, Paris, https://doi.org/10.1787/667fbe08-en. [12]

Alimujiang, A. et al. (2019), "Association between life purpose and mortality among US adults older than 50 years", *JAMA Network Open*, Vol. 2/5, https://doi.org/10.1001/JAMANETWORKOPEN.2019.4270. [55]

Alschuler, K., M. Jensen and D. Ehde (2012), "Defining mild, moderate, and severe pain in persons with multiple sclerosis", *Pain Medicine*, Vol. 13/10, pp. 1358-1365, https://doi.org/10.1111/j.1526-4637.2012.01471.x. [38]

Benjamin, D. et al. (2023), "Adjusting for scale-use heterogeneity in self-reported well-being", *SSRN Electronic Journal*, https://doi.org/10.2139/SSRN.4568587. [10]

Benjamin, D. et al. (2014), "Beyond happiness and satisfaction: Toward well-being indices based on stated preference", *The American Economic Review*, Vol. 104/9, pp. 2698-2735, https://doi.org/10.1257/AER.104.9.2698. [123]

Blanchflower, D. and A. Oswald (2019), "Unhappiness and pain in modern America: A review essay, and further evidence, on Carol Graham's Happiness for All?", *Journal of Economic Literature*, Vol. 57/2, pp. 385-402, https://doi.org/10.1257/JEL.20171492. [48]

BLS (2022), *American Time Use Survey (ATUS) Data Dictionary: 2021 Well-being Module Data Variables collected in the ATUS Well-being Module Important Information about the Well-being Module Data Dictionary*, U.S. Bureau of Labor Statistics, http://www.bls.gov/tus/wbmquestionnaire.pdf. [118]

Bohlmeijer, E. et al. (2023), "Spirituality in the context of well-being: Evaluation of the psychometric properties and added value of the Spiritual Attitude and Involvement List Short Form (SAIL-SF)", *Journal of Happiness Studies*, Vol. 24/3, pp. 1169-1190, https://doi.org/10.1007/s10902-023-00640-8. [131]

Bond, T. and K. Lang (2019), "The sad truth about happiness scales", *Journal of Political Economy*, Vol. 127/4, pp. 1629-1640, https://doi.org/10.1086/701679/SUPPL_FILE/2014587DATA.ZIP. [5]

Boyle, P. et al. (2009), "Purpose in life is associated with mortality among community-dwelling older persons", *Psychosomatic Medicine*, Vol. 71/5, pp. 574-579, https://doi.org/10.1097/PSY.0b013e3181a5a7c0. [56]

Case, A., A. Deaton and A. Stone (2020), "Decoding the mystery of American pain reveals a warning for the future", *Proceedings of the National Academy of Sciences of the United States of America*, Vol. 117/40, pp. 24785-24789, https://doi.org/10.1073/PNAS.2012350117. [21]

CBS (2024), *Centre for Bhutan Studies and GNH Research*, Centre for Bhutan Studies (CBS), https://bhutanstudies.org.bt/. [139]

Cella, D. et al. (2019), "PROMIS® Adult Health Profiles: Efficient Short-Form Measures of Seven Health Domains", *Value Health*, Vol. 22/5, pp. 537-544, https://doi.org/10.1016/J.JVAL.2019.02.004. [41]

Chen, Y. et al. (2019), "Sense of mission and subsequent health and well-being among young adults: An outcome-wide analysis", *American Journal of Epidemiology*, Vol. 188/4, pp. 664-673, https://doi.org/10.1093/AJE/KWZ009. [65]

Chou, E., B. Parmar and A. Galinsky (2016), "Economic insecurity increases physical pain", *Psychological Science*, Vol. 27/4, pp. 443-454, https://doi.org/10.1177/0956797615625640. [26]

Clarkson, L., V. Morrissette and G. Regallet (2001), *Our Responsibility to The Seventh Generation*, International Institute for Sustainable Development, https://www.iisd.org/publications/our-responsibility-seventh-generation. [150]

Cohen-Chen, S. and M. Van Zomeren (2018), "Yes we can? Group efficacy beliefs predict collective action, but only when hope is high", *Journal of Experimental Social Psychology*, Vol. 77, pp. 50-59, https://doi.org/10.1016/J.JESP.2018.03.016. [86]

Cohen, R., C. Bavishi and A. Rozanski (2016), "Purpose in life and its relationship to all-cause mortality and cardiovascular events: A meta-analysis", *Psychosomatic Medicine*, Vol. 78/2, pp. 122-133, https://doi.org/10.1097/PSY.0000000000000274. [57]

Correll, D. (2011), "The Measurement of Pain: Objectifying the Subjective", in Waldman, S. (ed.), *Pain Management*, W.B. Saunders, https://doi.org/10.1016/B978-1-4377-0721-2.00022-2. [32]

Cummins, R. (ed.) (2024), *Personal Wellbeing Index Manual*, Australian Centre on Quality of Life, School of Psychology, Deakin University – Melbourne Campus, https://www.acqol.com.au/uploads/pwi-a/pwi-a-english.pdf. [133]

Datta, R. (2023), "Indigenous Participatory Action Research (PAR)", in Okoko, J., S. Tunison and K. Walker (eds.), *Varieties of Qualitative Research Methods: Selected Contextual Perspectives*, Springer, Cham, https://doi.org/10.1007/978-3-031-04394-9_38. [161]

De Las Nueces, D. et al. (2012), "A systematic review of community-based participatory research to enhance clinical trials in racial and ethnic minority groups", *Health Services Research*, Vol. 47/3pt2, pp. 1363-1386, https://doi.org/10.1111/J.1475-6773.2012.01386.X. [166]

Deaton, A. (2012), "The financial crisis and the well-being of Americans", *Oxford Economic Papers*, Vol. 64/1, pp. 1-26, https://doi.org/10.1093/oep/gpr051. [47]

Diener, E., R. Lucas and S. Oishi (2002), "Subjective well-being: The science of happiness and life satisfaction", in Snyder, C. and S. Lopez (eds.), *Handbook of Positive Psychology*, Oxford University Press, https://psycnet.apa.org/record/2002-02382-005. [73]

Diener, E. et al. (2009), "New measures of well-being", *Social Indicators Research Series*, Vol. 39, pp. 247-266, https://doi.org/10.1007/978-90-481-2354-4_12. [137]

Edwards, L. et al. (2007), "Understanding hope: A review of measurement and construct validity research", *Oxford Handbook of Methods in Positive Psychology*, https://epublications.marquette.edu/edu_fac/407. [89]

Eisenberger, N. (2015), "Social pain and the brain: Controversies, questions, and where to go from here", *Annual Review of Psychology*, Vol. 66, pp. 601-629, https://doi.org/10.1146/annurev-psych-010213-115146. [15]

Eisenberger, N., M. Lieberman and K. Williams (2003), "Does rejection hurt? An FMRI study of social exclusion", *Science (New York, N.Y.)*, Vol. 302/5643, pp. 290-292, https://doi.org/10.1126/SCIENCE.1089134. [17]

European Union Agency for Fundamental Rights (2007), *EU Charter of Fundamental Rights*, Official Journal of the European Union, https://fra.europa.eu/en/eu-charter/article/1-human-dignity. [143]

Eurostat (2020), *Harmonised European Time Use Surveys : 2018 Guidelines : Re-edition, 2020 edition*, https://ec.europa.eu/eurostat/web/products-manuals-and-guidelines/-/ks-gq-20-011. [119]

Eurostat (2013), *2013 EU-SILC Module on Wellbeing: Assessment of the implementation*, https://ec.europa.eu/eurostat/documents/1012329/1012401/2013+Module+assessment.pdf. [70]

Exton, C., J. Mahoney and C. Smith (2024), "The OECD Guidelines on Measuring Subjective Well-being", in Brockmann, H. and R. Fernandez-Urbano (eds.), *Encyclopedia of Happiness, Quality of Life and Subjective Wellbeing*, Edward Elgar Publishing, https://doi.org/10.4337/9781800889675.00021. [4]

Fave, A. et al. (2016), "Lay definitions of happiness across nations: The primacy of inner harmony and relational connectedness", *Frontiers in Psychology*, Vol. 7/30, https://doi.org/10.3389/FPSYG.2016.00030. [148]

Fernandez, M. et al. (2017), "Special Issues in Conducting Community-Based Participatory Research Studies with Ethnic and Racial Minorities", in Coughlin, S., S. Smith and M. Fernandez (eds.), *Handbook of Community-Based Participatory Research*, Oxford University Press, https://doi.org/10.1093/ACPROF:OSO/9780190652234.003.0007. [162]

Gallup (n.d.), *Global Indicator: Emotional Wellbeing*, https://www.gallup.com/405494/indicator-global-emotional-wellbeing.aspx (accessed on 13 February 2025). [46]

Gallup World Poll (2024), *The State of Global Emotions*, https://www.gallup.com/analytics/349280/gallup-global-emotions-report.aspx. [141]

Gaskin, D. and P. Richard (2012), "The Economic Costs of Pain in the United States", *The Journal of Pain*, Vol. 13/8, pp. 715-724, https://doi.org/10.1016/J.JPAIN.2012.03.009. [24]

Geiger, N., T. Dwyer and J. Swim (2023), "Hopium or empowering hope? A meta-analysis of hope and climate engagement", *Frontiers in Psychology*, Vol. 14, p. 1139427, https://doi.org/10.3389/fpsyg.2023.1139427. [88]

Gilam, G. et al. (2020), "What is the relationship between pain and emotion? Bridging constructs and communities", *Neuron*, Vol. 107/1, pp. 17-21, https://doi.org/10.1016/J.NEURON.2020.05.024. [35]

Glei, D., A. Stokes and M. Weinstein (2020), "Changes in mental health, pain, and drug misuse since the mid-1990s: Is there a link?", *Social Science & Medicine*, Vol. 246, p. 112789, https://doi.org/10.1016/j.socscimed.2020.112789. [22]

Graham, C. (2024), *Hope, despair, and long-term outcomes*, https://www.brookings.edu/articles/hope-despair-and-long-term-outcomes/. [82]

Graham, C. and S. Pinto (2019), "Unequal hopes and lives in the USA: Optimism, race, place, and premature mortality", *Journal of Population Economics*, Vol. 32/2, pp. 665-733, https://www.jstor.org/stable/48699052. [76]

Graham, C. and J. Pozuelo (2023), "Do high aspirations lead to better outcomes? Evidence from a longitudinal survey of adolescents in Peru", *Journal of Population Economics*, Vol. 36/3, pp. 1099-1137, https://doi.org/10.1007/S00148-021-00881-Y. [84]

Griffiths, K. et al. (2021), "Indigenous and tribal peoples data governance in health research: A systematic review", *International Journal of Environmental Research and Public Health*, Vol. 18/19, p. 10318, https://doi.org/10.3390/IJERPH181910318. [163]

Hamby, S., J. Grych and V. Banyard (2013), *Life paths measurement packet: finalized Scales*, https://lifepathsresearch.org/wp-content/uploads/2021/10/Life-Paths-Measurement-Packet-finalized-scales-Aug-2015-Color-front-and-back.pdf. [134]

Hardy, S. and T. Schraepen (2024), "The state and effects of discrimination in the European Union", *OECD Papers on Well-being and Inequalities*, Vol. 26, https://doi.org/10.1787/7fd921b9-en. [145]

Hawker, G. et al. (2011), "Measures of adult pain", *Arthritis Care and Research*, Vol. 63/S11, pp. S240-S252, https://doi.org/10.1002/acr.20543. [30]

HealthMeasures (2021), *PROMIS Adult Profile Instruments*, https://www.healthmeasures.net/images/PROMIS/manuals/PROMIS_Adult_Profile_Scoring_Manual.pdf. [40]

Hill, P. et al. (2000), "Conceptualizing religion and spirituality: Points of commonality, points of departure", *Journal for the Theory of Social Behaviour*, Vol. 30/1, pp. 51-77, https://doi.org/10.1111/1468-5914.00119. [126]

Hill, P. and N. Turiano (2014), "Purpose in life as a predictor of mortality across adulthood", *Psychological Science*, Vol. 25/7, pp. 1482-1486, https://doi.org/10.1177/0956797614531799. [58]

Hirschfeld, G. and B. Zernikow (2013), "Variability of 'optimal' cut points for mild, moderate, and severe pain: Neglected problems when comparing groups", *Pain*, Vol. 154/1, pp. 154-159, https://doi.org/10.1016/J.PAIN.2012.10.008. [36]

Hoang, T. and A. Knabe (2021), "Time use, unemployment, and well-being: An empirical analysis using British time-use data", *Journal of Happiness Studies*, Vol. 22/6, pp. 2525-2548, https://doi.org/10.1007/s10902-020-00320-x. [109]

Human Flourishing Program (2024), *Spirituality & Flourishing*, Spirituality & Flourishing Interest Group: A part of the Flourishing Network in The Human Flourishing Program at Harvard University, https://www.spiritualflourishing.com/. [132]

Istat (2023), *Como uso il mio tempo: Indagine statistica multiscoppo sulle famiglie*, Istituto nazionale di statistica (Istat), https://siqual.istat.it/SIQual/files/IMF-13%20B%20Anno%202022-23.pdf?ind=0071301&cod=5591&progr=1&tipo=4. [116]

Jensen, M. and P. Karoly (2011), "Self-Report Scales and Procedures for Assessing Pain in Adults", in Turk, D. and R. Melzack (eds.), *Handbook of Pain Assessment*, The Guilford Press, https://psycnet.apa.org/record/2011-03491-002. [31]

Jensen, M. et al. (1999), "Comparative reliability and validity of chronic pain intensity measures", *Pain*, Vol. 83/2, pp. 157-162, https://doi.org/10.1016/S0304-3959(99)00101-3. [29]

Joshanloo, M. and A. Blasco-Belled (2023), "Reciprocal associations between depressive symptoms, life satisfaction, and eudaimonic well-being in older adults over a 16-year period", *International Journal of Environmental Research and Public Health*, Vol. 20/3, https://doi.org/10.3390/IJERPH20032374. [54]

Kaiser, C. and A. Oswald (2022), "The scientific value of numerical measures of human feelings", *PNAS*, Vol. 119/42, https://doi.org/10.1073/pnas.2210412119. [8]

Kaiser, C. and M. Vendrik (2020), "How threatening are transformations of happiness scales to subjective wellbeing research?", *IZA Discussion Paper*, No. 13905, Institute of Labor Economics, https://www.iza.org/publications/dp/13905/how-threatening-are-transformations-of-happiness-scales-to-subjective-wellbeing-research. [7]

Kant, S. et al. (2014), "Multi-domain subjective wellbeing of two Canadian First Nations communities", *World Development*, Vol. 64, pp. 140-157, https://doi.org/10.1016/J.WORLDDEV.2014.05.023. [167]

Karcioglu, O. et al. (2018), "A systematic review of the pain scales in adults: Which to use?", *The American Journal of Emergency Medicine*, Vol. 36/4, pp. 707-714, https://doi.org/10.1016/J.AJEM.2018.01.008. [33]

Kim, E., S. Hershner and V. Strecher (2015), "Purpose in life and incidence of sleep disturbances", *Journal of Behavioral Medicine*, Vol. 38/3, pp. 590-597, https://doi.org/10.1007/S10865-015-9635-4. [63]

Kim, E. et al. (2017), "Association between purpose in life and objective measures of physical function in older adults", *JAMA Psychiatry*, Vol. 74/10, pp. 1039-1045, https://doi.org/10.1001/JAMAPSYCHIATRY.2017.2145. [64]

Kim, E., V. Strecher and C. Ryff (2014), "Purpose in life and use of preventive health care services", *Proceedings of the National Academy of Sciences of the United States of America*, Vol. 111/46, pp. 16331-16336, https://doi.org/10.1073/PNAS.1414826111. [66]

Kim, E. et al. (2013), "Purpose in life and reduced risk of myocardial infarction among older U.S. adults with coronary heart disease: A two-year follow-up", *Journal of Behavioral Medicine*, Vol. 36/2, pp. 124-133, https://doi.org/10.1007/S10865-012-9406-4. [61]

Kim, E. et al. (2013), "Purpose in life and reduced incidence of stroke in older adults: 'The Health and Retirement Study'", *Journal of Psychosomatic Research*, Vol. 74/5, pp. 427-432, https://doi.org/10.1016/J.JPSYCHORES.2013.01.013. [62]

Kipuri, N. (2009), "Culture", in United Nations (ed.), *The State of the World's Indigenous Peoples*, Department of Economic and Social Affairs, https://doi.org/10.18356/532F27AC-EN. [156]

Klar, M. and T. Kasser (2009), "Some benefits of being an activist: Measuring activism and its role in psychological well-being", *Political Psychology*, Vol. 30/5, pp. 755-777, https://doi.org/10.1111/J.1467-9221.2009.00724.X. [87]

Koenig, H., M. McCullough and D. Larson (2001), *Handbook of Religion and Health*, Oxford University Press, https://psycnet.apa.org/record/2001-06078-000. [129]

Krekel, C. and G. MacKerron (2023), "Back to Edgeworth? Estimating the value of time using hedonic experiences", *IZA Discussion Paper* 16308, https://doi.org/10.2139/SSRN.4509724. [105]

Krekel, C. and G. MacKerron (2023), *Using people's feelings to value time*, What Works Wellbeing Centre, https://whatworkswellbeing.org/resources/using-peoples-feelings-to-value-time/. [113]

Krueger, A. et al. (2009), "National Time Accounting: The Currency of Life", in Krueger, A. (ed.), *Measuring the Subjective Well-Being of Nations: National Accounts of Time Use and Well-Being*, University of Chicago Press, https://www.nber.org/system/files/chapters/c5053/c5053.pdf. [117]

Krueger, A. and A. Mueller (2012), "Time use, emotional well-being, and unemployment: Evidence from longitudinal data", *American Economic Review*, Vol. 102/3, pp. 594-99, https://doi.org/10.1257/aer.102.3.594. [108]

Kruse, J. et al. (2008), "Survey of Living Conditions in the Arctic (SLiCA)", *Social Indicators Research Series*, Vol. 33, pp. 107-134, https://doi.org/10.1007/978-1-4020-8686-1_5. [164]

Kudrna, L. et al. (2024), "Measuring affective components of subjective well-being: Updated evidence to inform national data collections", *OECD Papers on Well-being and Inequalities*, No. 31, OECD Publishing, Paris, https://doi.org/10.1787/6c72da70-en. [11]

Lee, M., L. Kubzansky and T. VanderWeele (eds.) (2021), *Eudaimonic and hedonic well-being: An integrative perspective with linkages to sociodemographic factors and health*, Oxford University Press, https://doi.org/10.1093/OSO/9780197512531.003.0005. [97]

Leshem, O. (2019), "The pivotal role of the enemy in inducing hope for peace", *Political Studies*, Vol. 67/3, pp. 693-711, https://doi.org/10.1177/003232171879792. [85]

Lindqvist, E., R. Östling and D. Cesarini (2020), "Long-run effects of lottery wealth on psychological well-being", *The Review of Economic Studies*, Vol. 87/6, pp. 2703-2726, https://doi.org/10.1093/RESTUD/RDAA006. [9]

Liu, S. and N. Netzer (2023), "Happy times: Measuring happiness using response times", *American Economic Review*, Vol. 113/12, pp. 3289-3322, https://doi.org/10.1257/AER.20211051. [6]

Lomas, T. et al. (2022), "Balance and harmony in the Gallup World Poll: The development of the Global Wellbeing Initiative module", *International Journal of Wellbeing*, Vol. 12/4, pp. 1-19, https://doi.org/10.5502/IJW.V12I4.2655. [124]

Lomas, T. et al. (2022), "View of Balance and harmony in the Gallup World Poll: The development of the Global Wellbeing Initiative module", *International Journal of Wellbeing*, Vol. 4/12, pp. 1-19, https://www.internationaljournalofwellbeing.org/index.php/ijow/article/view/2655/1095. [146]

Lomas, T. et al. (2022), "Insights from the first global survey of balance and harmony", in Helliwell, J. et al. (eds.), *The World Happiness Report 2022*, Sustainable Development Solutions Network, New York, https://worldhappiness.report/ed/2022/insights-from-the-first-global-survey-of-balance-and-harmony/. [92]

Lomas, T. et al. (2025), "Differentiating balance and harmony through natural language analysis: A cross-national exploration of two understudied wellbeing-related concepts", *Journal of Positive Psychology*, https://doi.org/10.1080/17439760.2025.2459400. [147]

Long, K. et al. (2024), "Spirituality as a determinant of health: Emerging policies, practices, and systems", *Health Affairs (Project Hope)*, Vol. 43/6, pp. 783-790, https://doi.org/10.1377/HLTHAFF.2023.01643. [130]

Lumley, M. et al. (2011), "Pain and emotion: A biopsychosocial review of recent research", *Journal of Clinical Psychology*, Vol. 67/9, pp. 942-968, https://doi.org/10.1002/JCLP.20816. [34]

Lybbert, T. and B. Wydick (2018), "Poverty, aspirations, and the economics of hope", *Economic Development and Cultural Change*, Vol. 66/4, pp. 709-753, https://doi.org/10.1086/696968. [83]

Macchia, L. (2023), "Governments should measure pain when assessing societal wellbeing", *Nature Human Behaviour 2023 7:3*, Vol. 7/3, pp. 303-305, https://doi.org/10.1038/s41562-023-01539-3. [28]

Macchia, L. et al. (2025), "Physical pain as a component of subjective wellbeing", *Scientific Reports 2025 15:1*, Vol. 15/1, pp. 1-15, https://doi.org/10.1038/s41598-025-98421-1. [20]

Macchia, L. and A. Oswald (2021), "Physical pain, gender, and the state of the economy in 146 nations", *Social Science & Medicine*, Vol. 287, https://doi.org/10.1016/J.SOCSCIMED.2021.114332. [27]

Mahmoud, G., H. Rady and A. Mostafa (2019), "Cross-cultural adaptation and validation of an Arabic version of selected PROMIS measures for use in rheumatoid arthritis patients", *The Egyptian Rheumatologist*, Vol. 41/3, pp. 177-182, https://doi.org/10.1016/J.EJR.2018.09.003. [44]

Mahoney, J. (2023), "Subjective well-being measurement: Current practice and new frontiers", *OECD Papers on Well-being and Inequalities*, Vol. 17, https://doi.org/10.1787/4e180f51-en. [3]

Martela, F., E. Laitinen and C. Hakulinen (2024), "Which predicts longevity better: Satisfaction with life or purpose in life?", *Psychology and Aging*, Vol. 39/6, pp. 589-598, https://doi.org/10.1037/PAG0000802. [59]

Martela, F. and R. Ryan (2024), "Assessing autonomy, competence, and relatedness briefly: Validating single-item scales for basic psychological need satisfaction", *European Journal of Psychological Assessment*, https://doi.org/10.1027/1015-5759/A000846. [94]

Martela, F. and R. Ryan (2020), "Distinguishing between basic psychological needs and basic wellness enhancers: The case of beneficence as a candidate psychological need", *Motivation and Emotion*, Vol. 44/1, pp. 116-133, https://doi.org/10.1007/s11031-019-09800-x. [136]

Martela, F. and R. Ryan (2016), "The benefits of benevolence: Basic psychological needs, beneficence, and the enhancement of well-being", *Journal of Personality*, Vol. 84/6, pp. 750-764, https://doi.org/10.1111/JOPY.12215. [135]

Martikainen, S. et al. (2022), "Moments of meaningfulness and meaninglessness: A qualitative inquiry into affective eudaimonia at work", *Article Group & Organization Management*, Vol. 47/6, pp. 1135-1180, https://doi.org/10.1177/10596011211047324. [67]

McClintock, K. et al. (2021), "A collaboration to inform the development of an Indigenous wellbeing instrument", *Journal of Indigenous Wellbeing : Te mauri-Pimatisiwin*, Vol. 6/3, pp. 31-46, https://ndhadeliver.natlib.govt.nz/delivery/DeliveryManagerServlet?dps_pid=FL80078080. [168]

McClintock, K., G. Mellsop and T. Kingi (2011), "Development of a culturally attuned psychiatric outcome measure for an indigenous population", *International Journal of Culture and Mental Health*, Vol. 4/2, pp. 128-143, https://doi.org/10.1080/17542863.2010.537484. [157]

Mylona, E. (2023), *Learnings from time use data 2020-2021*, What Works Wellbeing Centre, https://doi.org/10.1177/0081175019884591. [107]

O'Connor, K. and C. Graham (2019), "Longer, more optimistic, lives: Historic optimism and life expectancy in the United States", *Journal of Economic Behavior & Organization*, Vol. 168, pp. 374-392, https://doi.org/10.1016/J.JEBO.2019.10.018. [77]

OECD (2025), *Social Connections and Loneliness in OECD Countries*, OECD Publishing, Paris, https://doi.org/10.1787/6df2d6a0-en. [114]

OECD (2024), *Bhutan's Gross National Happiness (GNH) Index*, https://www.oecd.org/en/publications/well-being-knowledge-exchange-platform-kep_93d45d63-en/bhutan-s-gross-national-happiness-gnh-index_ff75e0a9-en.html. [140]

OECD (2023), *Economic Policy Making to Pursue Economic Welfare: Report Prepared for the 2023 Japan Presidency of the G7*, OECD Publishing, Paris, https://www.oecd.org/economy/G7_Beyond_GDP_Economic_policy_making_to_pursue_economic_welfare_2023.pdf. [149]

OECD (2023), *How to Make Societies Thrive? Coordinating Approaches to Promote Well-being and Mental Health*, OECD Publishing, Paris, https://doi.org/10.1787/fc6b9844-en. [103]

OECD (2023), *Measuring Population Mental Health*, OECD Publishing, Paris, https://doi.org/10.1787/5171eef8-en. [102]

OECD (2013), *OECD Guidelines on Measuring Subjective Well-being*, OECD Publishing, Paris, https://doi.org/10.1787/9789264191655-en. [2]

OECD (forthcoming), *OECD Mental Health Data Pilot, 2025*, OECD Publishing, Paris. [104]

Oldenmenger, W. et al. (2013), "Cut points on 0–10 numeric rating scales for symptoms included in the Edmonton Symptom Assessment Scale in cancer patients: A systematic review", *Journal of Pain and Symptom Management*, Vol. 45/6, pp. 1083-1093, https://doi.org/10.1016/J.JPAINSYMMAN.2012.06.007. [37]

ONS (2024), *UK Measures of National Well-being Dashboard*, Office for National Statistics (ONS), https://www.ons.gov.uk/peoplepopulationandcommunity/wellbeing/articles/ukmeasuresofnationalwellbeing/dashboard. [91]

ONS (2011), *Initial Investigation into Subjective Well-being from the Opinions Survey*, Office for National Statistics (ONS), https://webarchive.nationalarchives.gov.uk/ukgwa/20160107223320/http:/www.ons.gov.uk/ons/rel/wellbeing/measuring-subjective-wellbeing-in-the-uk/investigation-of-subjective-well-being-data-from-the-ons-opinions-survey/initial-investigation-into-subjective-well-being-from-the-opinions-survey.html#tab-Section-7--Analysis-of-experience-subjective-well-being-questions--August-2011-. [50]

Panksepp, J. et al. (1978), "The biology of social attachments: Opiates alleviate separation distress", *Biol Psychiatry*, Vol. 13/5, pp. 607-618, https://pubmed.ncbi.nlm.nih.gov/83167/. [16]

Pavot, W. et al. (1991), "Further validation of the Satisfaction with Life Scale: Evidence for the cross-method convergence of well-being measures", *Journal of Personality Assessment*, Vol. 57/1, pp. 149-161, https://doi.org/10.1207/S15327752JPA5701_17. [74]

Peng-Keller, S. (2019), "Genealogies of spirituality: An historical analysis of a travelling term", *Journal for the Study of Spirituality*, Vol. 9/2, pp. 86-98, https://doi.org/10.1080/20440243.2019.1658261. [125]

Pérez Amador, A. (2025), *Desigualdades en el bienestar subjetivo en México: Brechas en el balance anímico según condiciones de salud y bienestar [Presentación de PowerPoint]*. [52]

Pérez Amador, A. (2023), "Balance anímico y brechas en el bienestar subjetivo de la población según condiciones de salud diversas", *Coyuntura Demográfica*, Vol. 22, https://coyunturademografica.somede.org/balance-animico-y-brechas-en-el-bienestar-subjetivo-de-la-poblacion-segun-condiciones-de-salud-diversas/ (accessed on 6 August 2025). [51]

Pleeging, E. (2022), "Measuring hope: Validity of short versions of four popular hope scales", *Quality and Quantity*, Vol. 56/6, pp. 4437-4464, https://doi.org/10.1007/S11135-022-01316-W. [90]

Prati, A. and C. Senik (2022), "Feeling good is feeling better", *Psychological Science*, Vol. 33/11, pp. 1828-1841, https://doi.org/10.1177/09567976221096158. [75]

Pritchard, A. et al. (2020), "The relationship between nature connectedness and eudaimonic well-being: A meta-analysis", *Journal of Happiness Studies*, Vol. 21/3, pp. 1145-1167, https://doi.org/10.1007/S10902-019-00118-6. [152]

Raja, S. et al. (2020), "The revised International Association for the Study of Pain definition of pain: concepts, challenges, and compromises", *Pain*, Vol. 161/9, pp. 1976-1982, https://doi.org/10.1097/J.PAIN.0000000000001939. [14]

Rawang, P. et al. (2020), "Cross-cultural adaptation, reliability, and construct validity of the Thai version of the Patient-Reported Outcomes Measurement Information System-29 in individuals with chronic low back pain", *Quality of Life Research*, Vol. 29/3, pp. 793-803, https://doi.org/10.1007/S11136-019-02363-X. [43]

Richardson, M. et al. (2021), "Moments, not minutes: The nature-wellbeing relationship", *International Journal of Wellbeing*, Vol. 11/1, pp. 8-33, https://doi.org/10.5502/IJW.V11I1.1267. [153]

Ringelheim, J. (2008), “Minority protection, data collection and the right to privacy”, *European Yearbook of Minority Issues*, Vol. 6/1, pp. 51-77, https://doi.org/10.1163/22116117-90001602. [160]

Russell, J. (1980), “A circumplex model of affect.”, *Journal of Personality and Social Psychology*, Vol. 39/6, pp. 1161-1178, https://doi.org/10.1037/h0077714. [93]

Rutherford, L. et al. (2024), *European Social Survey Round 12 Cognitive Interviewing*, National Centre for Social Research, https://europeansocialsurvey.org/sites/default/files/2025-04/natcen-ess12-cognitive-interviewing.pdf. [96]

Ryan, R. and E. Deci (2000), “Self-determination theory and the facilitation of intrinsic motivation, social development, and well-being”, *American Psychologist*, Vol. 55/1, pp. 68-78, https://doi.org/10.1037/0003-066X.55.1.68. [71]

Ryff, C. (2021), “Spirituality and well-being: Theory, science, and the nature connection”, *Religions*, Vol. 12/11, p. 914, https://doi.org/10.3390/REL12110914. [127]

Ryff, C. (2014), “Psychological well-being revisited: Advances in the science and practice of eudaimonia”, *Psychotherapy and Psychosomatics*, Vol. 83/1, pp. 10-28, https://doi.org/10.1159/000353263. [100]

Ryff, C. (1989), “Happiness is everything, or is it? Explorations on the meaning of psychological well-being”, *Journal of Personality and Social Psychology*, Vol. 57/6, pp. 1069-1081, https://doi.org/10.1037/0022-3514.57.6.1069. [72]

Ryff, C. and C. Keyes (1995), “The structure of psychological well-being revisited.”, *Journal of Personality and Social Psychology*, Vol. 69/4, pp. 719-727, https://doi.org/10.1037/0022-3514.69.4.719. [98]

Salazar, G., K. Kunkle and M. Monroe (2020), *Practitioner Guide to Assessing Connection to Nature*, North American Association for Environmental Education, Washington, DC, https://naaee.org/sites/default/files/2022-10/Assessing%20Connection%20to%20Nature.5.6.20.pdf. [154]

Serlin, R. et al. (1995), “When is cancer pain mild, moderate or severe? Grading pain severity by its interference with function”, *Pain*, Vol. 61/2, pp. 277-284, https://doi.org/10.1016/0304-3959(94)00178-H. [39]

Sharma, S. et al. (2021), “Translation and cross-cultural adaptation of Nepali versions of the Patient-Reported Outcomes Measurement Information System (PROMIS®) Pain Intensity, Pain Interference, Pain Behavior, Depression, and Sleep Disturbance short forms in chronic musculoskeletal pain”, *Quality of Life Research*, Vol. 30/4, pp. 1215-1224, https://doi.org/10.1007/S11136-020-02745-6. [42]

Smith, C. (2023), “The value of urban green space: An application of experienced wellbeing measures to cost-wellbeing analysis”, in *Experienced wellbeing, income, and measurement of the value of non-market outcomes*, Te Herenga Waka—Victoria University of Wellington, https://openaccess.wgtn.ac.nz/articles/thesis/Experienced_wellbeing_income_and_measurement_of_the_value_of_non-market_outcomes_/24240040?file=42552454. [106]

Smith, C. et al. (2025), “Globally inclusive measures of subjective wellbeing: Updated evidence to inform national data collections”, *OECD Papers on Well-being and Inequalities*, Vol. 35, https://doi.org/10.1787/bd72752a-en (accessed on 11 February 2025). [13]

Smith, C., E. Peach and J. Cording (2019), *The impact of multiple disadvantage on subjective wellbeing: New Zealand families*, Kōtātā Insight: Behavioural Economic & Social Analysis, https://msd.govt.nz/documents/about-msd-and-our-work/publications-resources/research/impact-of-multiple-disadvantage/the-impact-of-multiple-disadvantage-on-subjective-wellbeing.pdf. [122]

Snyder, C. (2000), "The past and possible futures of hope", *Journal of Social and Clinical Psychology*, Vol. 19/1, pp. 11-28, https://doi.org/10.1521/JSCP.2000.19.1.11. [79]

Statistics Canada (2022), *Time Use Survey - 2022: Questionnaire(s)*, Statistics Canada, https://www23.statcan.gc.ca/imdb/p3Instr.pl?Function=getInstrumentList&Item_Id=1395477&UL=1V. [115]

Statistics Finland (2024), *Citizens' Pulse*, Statistics Finland, https://stat.fi/en/surveys/pulssi. [95]

Statistics New Zealand (2023), *About the General Social Survey*, Statistics New Zealand, https://www.stats.govt.nz/help-with-surveys/list-of-stats-nz-surveys/about-the-general-social-survey/. [120]

Statistics New Zealand (2014), *Te Kupenga 2013 (English)*, Statistics New Zealand, https://www.stats.govt.nz/information-releases/te-kupenga-2013-english. [121]

Steger, M. et al. (2008), "Understanding the search for meaning in life: personality, cognitive style, and the dynamic between seeking and experiencing meaning", *Journal of Personality*, Vol. 76/2, pp. 199-228, https://doi.org/10.1111/J.1467-6494.2007.00484.X. [68]

Steptoe, A. and D. Fancourt (2019), "Leading a meaningful life at older ages and its relationship with social engagement, prosperity, health, biology, and time use", *Proceedings of the National Academy of Sciences*, Vol. 116/4, pp. 1207-1212, https://doi.org/10.1073/pnas.1814723116. [60]

Stiglitz, J., A. Sen and J. Fitoussi (2009), *Report by the Commission on the Measurement of Economic Performance and Social Progress*, https://ec.europa.eu/eurostat/documents/8131721/8131772/Stiglitz-Sen-Fitoussi-Commission-report.pdf. [1]

Stone, A. and C. Mackie (eds.) (2013), *Subjective Well-Being: Measuring Happiness, Suffering, and Other Dimensions of Experience*, The National Academies Press, Committee on National Statistics, Division of Behavioral and Social Sciences and Education. Washington, DC, https://doi.org/10.17226/18548. [19]

Takahashi, H. et al. (2009), "When your gain is my pain and your pain is my gain: Neural correlates of envy and schadenfreude", *Science (New York, N.Y.)*, Vol. 323/5916, pp. 937-939, https://doi.org/10.1126/SCIENCE.1165604. [18]

Tchipeva, T., M. Miceli and E. Ninka (2024), *Time Use Surveys in Europe: State of play and a glimpse into the future*, Eurostat, https://unstats.un.org/unsd/demographic-social/meetings/2024/tus-egm-20240130/Session-2B-c-Eurostat-Eniel-Ninka.pdf (accessed on 14 February 2025). [112]

Tremolada, M. et al. (2020), "Psychological wellbeing in adolescents with leukaemia: A comparative study with typical development peers", *International Journal of Environmental Research and Public Health*, Vol. 17/2, p. 567, https://doi.org/10.3390/IJERPH17020567. [78]

Tuhiwai Smith, L. (2021), “Introduction”, in *Decolonizing Methodologies*, Zed Books, https://www.bloomsbury.com/us/decolonizing-methodologies-9781786998125/. [158]

U.S. Bureau of Labor Statistics (2022), *American Time Use Survey Well-being Module Questionnaire*, U.S. Bureau of Labor Statistics, https://www.bls.gov/tus/questionnaires/wbmquestionnaire.pdf. [49]

UN (2015), *Transforming Our World: The 2030 Agenda for Sustainable Development*, United Nations Department of Economic and Social Affairs Sustainable Development, https://sdgs.un.org/2030agenda. [144]

UN (1948), *Universal Declaration of Human Rights*, United Nations, https://www.un.org/en/about-us/universal-declaration-of-human-rights. [142]

United Nations (2023), *Protecting minority rights: A practical guide to developing comprehensive anti-discrimination legislation*, UN Office of the High Commissioner for Human Rights, https://digitallibrary.un.org/record/4009265. [159]

United Nations (2018), “Indigenous peoples and ethnic minorities: Marginalization is the norm”, in *Promoting Inclusion through Social Protection*, United Nations, https://www.un.org/development/desa/dspd/wp-content/uploads/sites/22/2018/07/Chapter-VIIIndigenous-peoples-and-ethnic-minorities.pdf. [155]

UNSD (2025), *Guide to Producing Statistics on Time Use*, United Nations Statistics Division, https://unstats.un.org/UNSDWebsite/statcom/session_55/documents/BG-3k-Guide_to_Producing_Statistics_on_Time_Use-55UNSC_background-E.pdf. [111]

Ura, K. et al. (2022), *GNH 2022*, Centre for Bhutan & GNH Studies, Thimphu, Bhutan, https://ophi.org.uk/sites/default/files/2024-03/Bhutan_GNH_2022_%282023%29_compressed.pdf. [138]

Ura, K., S. Alkire and T. Zangmo (2012), “Case Study: Bhutan Gross National Happiness and the GNH Index”, in Helliwell, J., R. Layard and J. Sachs (eds.), *World Happiness Report*, Columbia Earth Institute. The Earth Institute, Columbia University, New York, https://worldhappiness.report/ed/2012/ (accessed on 5 March 2025). [151]

UW Madison (2025), *MIDUS – Midlife in the United States*, University of Wisconsin-Madison, https://midus.wisc.edu/. [101]

van den Berg, M. et al. (2024), “PaRIS Field Trial Report: Technical report on the international PaRIS survey of people living with chronic conditions”, *OECD Health Working Papers*, No. 166, OECD Publishing, Paris, https://doi.org/10.1787/e5725c75-en. [45]

van Dierendonck, D. (2012), “Spirituality as an essential determinant for the good life, its importance relative to self-determinant psychological needs”, *Journal of Happiness Studies*, Vol. 13/4, pp. 685-700, https://doi.org/10.1007/S10902-011-9286-2. [128]

Ward, G. (2019), “Happiness and voting behavior”, in Helliwell, J., R. Layard and J. Sachs (eds.), *World Happiness Report 2019*, Sustainable Development Solutions Network, New York, https://worldhappiness.report/ed/2019/happiness-and-voting-behavior/. [80]

Ward, G. et al. (2021), “(Un)happiness and voting in U.S. presidential elections”, *Journal of Personality and Social Psychology*, Vol. 120/2, pp. 370-383, https://doi.org/10.1037/PSPI0000249. [81]

Waterman, A. et al. (2010), "The questionnaire for eudaimonic well-being: Psychometric properties, demographic comparisons, and evidence of validity", *The Journal of Positive Psychology*, Vol. 5/1, pp. 41-61, https://doi.org/10.1080/17439760903435208. [99]

Wenig, C. et al. (2009), "Costs of back pain in Germany", *European Journal of Pain*, Vol. 13/3, pp. 280-286, https://doi.org/10.1016/J.EJPAIN.2008.04.005. [23]

What Works Wellbeing (2021), *What matters for our sense of purpose?*, What Works Wellbeing Centre, https://whatworkswellbeing.org/resources/sense-of-purpose-covid/. [69]

WHO (2022), *Mental Health*, World Health Organization, https://www.who.int/news-room/fact-sheets/detail/mental-health-strengthening-our-response. [53]

Wiech, K. and I. Tracey (2009), "The influence of negative emotions on pain: Behavioral effects and neural mechanisms", *NeuroImage*, Vol. 47/3, pp. 987-994, https://doi.org/10.1016/J.NEUROIMAGE.2009.05.059. [25]

Wolf, T. et al. (2019), "Experienced well-being and labor market status: The role of pleasure and meaning", *SOEPpapers on Multidisciplinary Panel Data Research*, https://EconPapers.repec.org/RePEc:diw:diwsop:diw_sp1043. [110]

Wu, F. (2021), "Modern economic growth, culture, and subjective well-being: Evidence from Arctic Alaska", *Journal of Happiness Studies*, Vol. 22/6, pp. 2621-2651, https://doi.org/10.1007/S10902-020-00335-4. [165]

www.ingramcontent.com/pod-product-compliance
Lightning Source LLC
LaVergne TN
LVHW060454061126
851857LV00016B/1821
9789264720046